Anna Mancini, Ph. D

How to unlock
the secrets, enigmas, and mysteries of
Ancient Egypt
and other old civilizations

Buenos Books America

www.buenosbooks.us

All rights reserved.
© 2007-2008 Anna MANCINI

No part of this book may be reproduced, stored in a retrieval system, or transmitted by any means, electronic, mechanical, photocopying, recording, or otherwise, without written permission from the author.

ISBN: 978-1-932848-59-5 (PAPERBACK)

Previously published as :
How To Better Understand Ancient Civilizations.

English and Spanish versions published by:
BUENOS BOOKS AMERICA
info@buenosbooks.us
http://www.buenosbooks.us

French version published by:
Buenos Books International (Paris)
www.BuenosBooks.fr
info@BuenosBooks.fr

AUTHOR'S WEBSITE

http://www.amancini.com

To :

Antonietta Caraccio and Lorenzo Mancini,
With gratitude.

Anna

CONTENTS

PRELIMINARY CHAPTER   7
My special path to the study of ancient civilizations

CHAPTER 1   27
Exploring the functioning of your body at the meeting point between dreams and reality

CHAPTER 2   47
An efficient method for observing the connections between your dreams and your reality

CHAPTER 3   81
The world you will discover through the dream reality work

CHAPTER 4   107
A powerful technique for accessing information stored in your unconscious

CHAPTER 5   115
The best conditions to be helped by your unconscious for your research about ancient civilizations
CONCLUSION   133

| BIBLIOGRAPHY | 135 |
| NOTES | 137 |

PRELIMINARY CHAPTER

My special path to the study of ancient civilizations

Taranto, a south Italian city, was founded around 706 A. D. by a Greek Spartan colony. However, modern visitors to the city will only find two temple columns remaining from the ancient Greek temple that was once erected in this beautiful site, facing the deep blue of the ocean. My parents lived in the former sacred area of this old temple. It is there that I was conceived a short time before they left their country for France, where I was born.

Even though modern psychology has evidenced the reality of psychic transgenerational heredity, the facts that I was conceived in this ancient place and am a descendant of remote Greek ancestors were not enough to help me gain a better understanding of the ancient Mediterranean civilizations. Other sets of circumstances were required. The first was brought to me by my parents. My father was a "normal" man for his time. He was rational and logical. He was literate and could quickly adapt to the culture and language of his new adoptive country. The mental structure of my mother was thoroughly different. Due to a significant hearing impairment, my mother could not go to school and was illiterate. Because of these circumstances, her mind remained almost untouched by the influences of the modern world. She grew up in a different world—a world created mainly from images, physical sensations, and intuitions, where reading and writing were absent. She used her brain differently and developed an unusual kind of intelligence that gave little room for our much valued modern rationality and no room at all for our abstractions. My mother's mental structure was more similar to those of ancient peoples who were considered to have pre-logical minds. Later in my life, I understood that my mother had been an open book for me on the mental universe of ancient Mediterranean peoples and that she had prepared me to better understand the laws and the minds of the ancient civilizations that I was to study at the university. My father spoke Italian and French, but my mother only spoke the old Taranto's dialect. It was this old language full of images that became my mother tongue. Later on, in the course of studying archaic Roman law, the knowledge of this old language helped me a great deal. However, before arriving at this stage in my life, I had to go through a long patient route in my family life. My parents lived in two different and disconnected universes of thought. By observing them, I realized that they were both intelligent, but possessed different kinds of intelligence. My father and my mother enacted the encounter between ancient and modern worlds, between the logical modern universe and the pre-logical universe of older civilizations. Obviously, my mother was so lonely in her world. To help her, I began translating French newspapers, books, movies, and conversations for her, speaking as loud as I could. In my early childhood, I had developed French-Italian dialect interpretation skills, but more importantly (and more difficult), I had learned to translate things and concepts from our universe of thought into my mother's pre-logical universe of thought. In order to better communicate with her, I entered step-by-step into her world. There, I could discover a different rationality, another way to conceive time and space, a different approach to communicate with others, an intense dream activity, a vivid imagination, a powerful intuition and a strong sense of reality that I did not notice in other people around me. Little by little, I realized that my mother's brain was extremely active, giving her an intense "inner life" that filled her with a great joy that she passed to everybody around her. Many times, I noticed that what my mother said had to be "translated" into the language of our conscious mind in order to be properly understood. I had the clear feeling that my mother's psyche was tuned into life, energy, nature and the cosmos. It is this same "feeling" that I experienced later on in my life when I visited museums of antiquity. My father's psyche, to the contrary, was focused on the external world and the concerns of daily life. He had no interest in dreams and did not have the "antennas" which my mother strongly used in her life and which she used one day to save my life. Thanks to my father, and then thanks to the schools of Cartesian France, I developed my "modern" mind. At the same time, through my mother, I learned to communicate with my own inner pre-logical world or the ancient layers of my psyche that are richly alive during the dream process but unconscious for the most part during my waking state. My mother taught me how to use dreams to better manage my waking life. As I explored my inner world, I came to realize that our modern rational and logical mental universe is only a tiny iceberg floating over the immensely rich psychic ocean that was well-known to ancient civilizations. For most of us, this ocean does not exist. However at night, in our dreams, we all return to it.

When I was twenty years old, I left my family in order to study the law at the University of Lille (North of France). There, everybody had a "normal mind". Cautiously, I limited myself to their mental universe. There was nobody with whom I could share this other rich and more alive dimension of the psyche. Little by little, I forgot my mother's world. For the study of law I had no need of imagination, dreams, intuition, and the pre-logical way of thinking. My old dialect was useless, too. Who would speak this language there? Nobody. I was studying civil law and planning to become a barrister and a professor of law. My cultural heritage took me to a completely different destiny.

My second encounter with the ancient worlds took place in my fourth year of studies. All of this began with the choice to study Roman law. It was an optional matter and I enrolled in it, following my intuition and not listening to my conscious mind telling me it would be useless for my career as a lawyer in business law. How gladly surprised I was to notice that in archaic Roman law the universe of thought was very similar to my mother's. This made me so happy and curious. I felt close to this ancient system and familiar with it. It was amazing that such an old legal system was still taught in universities and still fully alive through all the continental legal systems. Our professor of Roman law was a "celebrity" from the University of Paris. Each week he would come to Lille to share, with much enthusiasm and passion, his scholarly knowledge about Roman law. The knowledge he was passing to us taught me much more than what he could himself grasp, because I was much better trained than him to understand this ancient universe of thought. While this intelligent man laughed at these "primitive" people because he did not understand them, he was opening doors for me that had stayed perfectly closed to all the specialists that had approached the archaic Roman law with their modern minds. I understood that this "law" was, in fact, an unexplored source of knowledge about the intangible world and about the human brain. Thanks to my different approach to Roman law, later, during my doctoral research at the University of Paris, I was glad to bring to the academic circle (in its language) the solution to the famous enigma of ancient Roman law, which was called the enigma of rights. This issue gave place to abundant research and jurisprudence, which lead to nowhere to such an extent that after several centuries of research performed by the most eminent European scholars, it was decided to abandon this fruitless quest.

This discovery did not please my thesis supervisor, a powerful member of the University of Paris and a French academician. He did everything he could to block the circulation of my work and barred me from the university. When this man retired from the university, I returned for a second thesis about the philosophy of Internet law under the direction of a friendly Greek philosopher. Surprisingly, these new researches lead me to my third encounter with ancient civilizations. This time it was ancient Egypt. How did Internet law bring me to ancient Egypt? The fact is that I had realized that the Aristotelian concept of justice (and its derived modern versions) was conceived for a tangible world but was useless within the Internet. As I researched a concept of justice that would be suited to the Internet (an intangible world), I found books and articles about Maat, the ancient Egyptian concept of justice.

Between my two doctoral theses ten years had elapsed, during which I had gone to the University of London where I studied the philosophy of the mind. During this time, I had also founded *Innovative You*, a Paris-based research organization on the functioning of the creative mind. I created this organization because as I was working as a lawyer in the field of patent law, I met many inventors who dreamed their innovative ideas and I wanted to understand this phenomenon in order to provoke it at will, instead of waiting for its random occurrence. In the frame of this organization I performed a lot of experiments, deepened my research on the mind, and taught many people. From this work resulted the invention of a method that I still teach today to people wanting to access and use their unconscious intelligence. This method also allows one to be in touch again with the ancient layers of our psyche, which helps to better understand how our remote ancestors perceived the world surrounding them.

Thanks to all the experience I gained, I realized while I was doing research about Maat, the ancient goddess of justice, how much Egyptologists would need to practice my method in order to be able to benefit from the now abundant remains of the ancient Egyptian civilization. It was obvious that, as they studied these archeological remains with their modern minds, they could not understand the concept of Maat. Moreover, they had made a lot of mistakes regarding the meaning of ancient Egyptian images, which sometimes made me smile. (I apologize!) For example, take Ammit (also called Amut, Ammat, and Ahemait), which Egyptologists translate into: "the great devourer", "the devourer", "the big eater", "the gobbler", "the eater of bones", "the eater of millions", etc. Here is an image of Ammit:

You can see that Ammit is an animal formed with the parts of different other animals: a crocodile head with a wide open jaw and big teeth, the rear of a hippopotamus, and the chest of a lion (or leopard), and probably the mane of a lion. Here Ammit is in its most usual context at the bottom of the scales; this image is frequently found on funerary papyri or painted on coffins and carved on walls.

I made this drawing after the papyrus of Hunefer, an Egyptian scribe who lived around 1310 BC. The papyrus belongs to the British Museum in London. It is interesting to see the original image, as its colors and theme strongly impress our unconscious mind. The original image is easy to find on the Internet through a search with the following key words : weighing of the heart, psychostasy, or judgment of the dead.

Here are some links :

www.siloam.net/rostau/ newgiza/entrance.html;

www.guardians.net/hawass/ tomb_of_iuf-aa.htm;

http://web.ukonline.co.uk/gavin.egypt).

Here are some quotes showing how scholars perceive Ammit:

> *If the verdict should be unfavorable, the sinner falls victim to 'the devourer'.... a hybrid monster...*[1]
>
> *Ammit the monster perches on a shrine-shaped plinth before a heaped table of offerings ready to gobble down any heart weighed down by sin.*[2]
>
> *Thoth stands ready to write down the result, watched by the monster Ammit, who gobbles down hearts laden with sin.*[3]

A monster looking like a hippopotamus, the Devourer, is sat near the scales waiting to receive the heart of the damned sinner.[4]

After the Armanian era, the image of the "Devourer" representing the jaw of hell will be added.[5]

Amam (Ammit) is depicted as a composite beast, awaiting the results of the weighing of the heart in the Hall of Judgment. The heart symbolizes consciousness. Those hearts that weigh more than the feather of truth are thrown to Amam.[6]

His heart is judged by the scales of divine justice. If it is heavier than a feather of Maat, the goddess of Truth, the dead man is thrown to the monster Ammit, who devours the deceased with his crocodile jaws. Ammit had a crocodile head; his body was part lion and part hippopotamus.[7]

If Ani's heart is heavier than the feather, he will not be allowed to enter the afterlife. In fact, he will be destroyed by a hideous monster -Ammit, the Devourer. This 'eater of the dead' stands just behind Thoth, ready to pounce. It has the head of a crocodile, the forequarters of a lion, and the hindquarters of a hippopotamus.[8]

Souls that failed to pass were devoured by Ammit, one of the more fantastic of mythological creatures. At the trial he stood near Anubis, eager for the tasty dish that was his should the soul fail the test. He was a composite of three ferocious animals: he had the head of a crocodile, the body

> *of a lion, and the backside of a hippopotamus; his name meant "eater of the dead.*[9]

Before you read what follows, why not try to understand Ammit and also the scene from the papyrus of Hunefer? What is its atmosphere? The specialists have called the scene "the judgment of the dead", the "weighing of the heart", and the "psychostasy". Do not let these labels influence your mind. Try to look at the scene with new eyes and with your whole sensitivity. What emotions does it trigger in you? What is Ammit for? Look at it. Are you afraid? Are the characters in the scene afraid of it? Why is this named Ammit? Try to understand.

As we can see from the quotes, Ammit is commonly perceived as a monster in charge of eating the sinner who could not pass the test of the weighing of the heart. This mistake is repeated everywhere by everybody, because the modern mind can only see Ammit as a "monster". If scholars had been trained in understanding their symbolic dream language they would not have made this regrettable mistake, which, by the same token, barred them from understanding the concept of Maat. Maat is a key concept; understanding it allows answering many other unresolved questions about the ancient Egyptian civilization. This also helps improve the translation of many ancient Egyptian texts.

An author wondered why Ammit the monster is in every picture of the judgment of the dead. The answer to this question is very easy.

According to my experience, it is clear that Ammit is not a monster but only the way the ancient Egyptian priests found to represent their scientific knowledge of the death process. Ammit stands for death. To understand it, we need to actually look at ancient images instead of promptly tacking on them our preconceived ideas and judgments. In the ancient image of the scene of justice, for example, we are actually far from the atmosphere of judgments, sins, fear, and guilty feelings of the Judeo-Christian world. This scene does not picture a judgment, not even a weighing, but something else, as I explain in detail in my book on Maat. As for Ammit, it is no coincidence that its name is "the devourer". What other than death gobbles down everybody? (This is why Ammit also means "eater of millions".) Sinner or not, guilty or not, Ammit will decompose your body and in this process will make it disappear. Reading this image as if it were an image emerging from the unconscious, it is possible to access the ancient Egyptian knowledge about the process of death, when the conscious mind is only afraid of a horrible monster! Once properly deciphered, the symbol Ammit in its context says that the ancient Egyptians had observed that death occurs when there is not a correct circulation of Maat in the body (life energy coming from the sun), which involves disharmony (hence the disharmonious animal) that provokes the decomposition of the body (hence the composite body of the animal) and the disappearance of the body (hence the open jaw that eats all and makes all disappear). Why would the ancient Egyptians amuse themselves by representing a monster in a scene that, as a whole, was so peaceful? Compared to Ammit, our modern skeleton with its scythe is a poor explanation of the process of death and of physical decay!

When we understand through a symbolic reading that the scene of the "judgment of the dead" is not at all a "judgment of the dead", but a symbolic representation of natural processes, we can answer the question that was raised about the presence of Ammit in every picture of the judgment of the dead. The answer is: there is an excellent reason from the Egyptian point of view to always picture this "monster" in this scene, which, as a whole, shows the process of life and the process of death. The contrast shown between life and death in the same symbolic image enriches the meaning of the whole picture. It is remarkable to notice that in one picture alone, the ancient Egyptians were able to convey to the people able to "read" it their knowledge about the way life is sustained and the way death occurs when life if no longer sustained. If we make a comparison with modern technology, this image is like a compressed file that needs a "primitive mind" to be opened and decompressed, but that cannot be opened by the conscious mind alone.

Through the striking example of Ammit as a symbol, though easy to decipher due to the fact that the ancient Egyptians had given it an explicit name, it is easy to understand the great advantage that scholars could draw from a proper training in understanding their dream symbols using the easy method I explain in this book.

Dealing with archaeological remains from ancient civilizations with a modern matter-oriented mind is time wasted. Our modern mental structure does not make it at all possible to enter the logic of ancient peoples who explored better than us the intangible side of life. We ignore this aspect of life, but it is nevertheless perceived by our bodies, which transmit information about it to our brain through dreams. The best way to be closer to this ancient people's state of mind is to rediscover in our inner world the ancient layers of our psyche that are richly alive in the dream process. You can do it applying the method I explain in the next chapter. This method will also be profitable to train researchers to actually look at ancient images and symbols instead of being prisoners of their conscious minds, projecting preconceived ideas and impeding them to actually look at what is under their eyes. The dream reality method is a valuable tool to help train the conscious mind to cooperate better with the unconscious and to get more from its information wealth. Through observing the connections between your dreams and your reality, you will also access the mental universe and understand the special sensitivity of ancient peoples in regard to the environmental energies that we no longer perceive in the waking state. Why? The fact is that when we sleep, our dream consciousness is fully focused on the management of life energy and on the intangible links we build with each other. These were also the main concerns of ancient people in their waking life, which we can only remember in the dream state. When you discover your dream world and its connection to the real world, you will understand how the ancient peoples perceived their universe, tangible and intangible. This will help you understand all that usually looks "primitive" under the angle of modern man, who has considerably lost his capacity to physically sense environmental energies. Modern man has so much lost this capacity to perceive the energy side of life that he only pays attention to the material world, the sole reality he can now consciously perceive. However, the ancient people could perceive much better than us the energies of nature. They had explored the laws of the intangible world and had observed that our body functions as a natural bridge between the tangible and the intangible worlds. Proof of such knowledge can be found particularly in ancient legal systems like archaic Roman law. The knowledge I have gained through the study of this ancient legal system and through my dream reality work has inspired the first chapter of this book, where I explain the functioning of the body at the meeting point between dreams and reality and the importance to observe this phenomenon in order to understand the dream process.

In the second chapter of this book, I will explain a method you can use to efficiently explore your psyche and reach its ancient layers, which are closely linked to instinct, nature, and reality.

In the third chapter, I will speak about the results that can be achieved by almost anyone after one year of dream reality work. Through these results you will see the ancient mental universe of your remote ancestors emerge. You will come to understand many of their striking attitudes; for example, why they were so keen on oracles and on anticipating the future.

In the fourth chapter, I will explain a technique that you will be able to use once you have decoded your own dream symbols. This technique will allow you to get, at will, information from your unconscious. It can be used in any field, even to find lost things.

In the fifth and last chapter, I list some of the best conditions for fruitful cooperation between the conscious and the unconscious mind.

CHAPTER 1

Exploring the functioning of your body at the meeting point between dreams and reality

In the modern Western world almost everybody has lost the ability to consciously perceive the intangible world that surrounds us. This ability was part of the survival instinct of the first human beings and the ancient layers of our psyche have kept traces of it. For example, we are unable to perceive the harmonious or disharmonious energy of places, people, or objects. However, our body is still influenced by the energies around it. Through the study of the connections between your dream and your reality, you will be aware of this intangible reality to which the ancient people were extremely sensitive. This is because you will see that your body permanently sends to your brain, through the dream channel, information about the energy of places, people, and objects that it has picked up but that no longer reach our waking life consciousness. This is why I now propose for you to study the functioning of your body at the meeting point between your dreams and your reality.

If you want to understand the dream process, it is necessary to go beyond the dream itself. If you consider dreams in the physical and invisible environment in which they have occurred, it is possible to observe the role played by the human body at the meeting point between dreams and reality. Let us start with the observation of the natural environment where dreams occur.

When observing life upon earth, we can notice the existence of two kinds of reality: what we can call a "material" or a "tangible world" and what we can call an "immaterial" or an "intangible" world. The material world is made of everything we can touch, see, or move, for example a flower, a chair, a boat, a house and also the human body. The intangible world is composed of intangible things, like ideas, emotions, scents but also the human mind, which we cannot see or touch. We can schematically represent these observations in the following diagram:

Diagram n° 1:

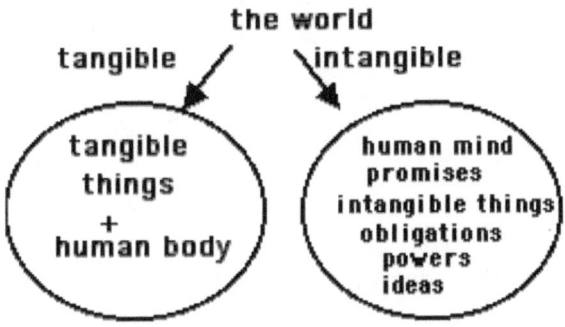

However, this diagram is not fully correct. Obviously the material and the immaterial worlds are not disconnected. On the contrary, they are interwoven and in constant interaction, and this is particularly true for human beings. This reality is what Sören Kierkegaard wanted to express when he wrote: "Man is a synthesis of finite and infinite."[10] We can, therefore, draw a more accurate diagram of the environment in which dreams occur:

Diagram n° 2:

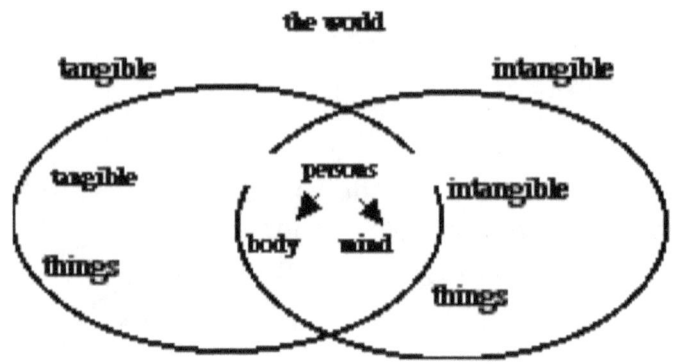

Through this diagram we can clearly understand that human beings through their bodies pertain to the material world, while with their minds, thoughts, feelings, emotions, odors and so on, they belong to the intangible world. In other words, human beings appear to be a natural bridge between the tangible and the intangible. Societies we generally consider to be primitive did not fail to notice this important aspect of human life. They took this truth into consideration in their philosophy of life and in some cases in their legal systems.

Our modern civilization, being mainly focused on the material world, shows a great ignorance and a great contempt toward many areas of the intangible world.

Because of this we know very little about the functioning of the intangible world and we ignore, for example, the following fundamental rule of the intangible world:

In order to act upon the intangible world, we always need a tangible means and the human body is an excellent means to reach the intangible. Through the body everyone is a natural bridge between the material and the intangible worlds. It is impossible to reach directly the intangible. We can do it only through matter--like our bodies.

In the same way, it is impossible to directly act upon ideas, which are also intangible realities. However, this does not prevent us from transmitting them through speech, books or computers. Generally speaking, we deny the reality of all the intangible things (and also of some tangible things) that we are unable to perceive. If, for example, we were unable to sense odors, they would not exist for us. Every person lives in his/her own unique reality composed of all the realities he/she senses and accepts. The reality accepted by the Western world is very different from the reality that is accepted by so-called primitive tribes. In order to admit the existence of realities we cannot perceive (for example the existence of a foreign country we have never visited), we must trust the people who speak or write about this reality. Though we are unable to perceive them, we admit their existence. We have accepted that they form part of our own reality.

Sometimes it can be very hard to explain to someone a reality that we know very well, but that does not exist in our interlocutor's world. **In such a case we make use of everything known by this person to help describe this new reality and have it accepted.** This is what often occurs with dreams.

Every night, dreams convey to our conscious mind some information from the environment (immediate or remote) that is picked up by the body but not by the conscious mind (focused on its own reality). In our environment, much more information is available than what the conscious mind receives. For example, information regarding the vitality of all living beings is not available to the conscious mind, which will remember mainly the physical aspects of the living beings. **Dreams are a**

means for accessing an important source of information that the conscious mind, in our state of mental development, is unable to perceive.

The actual perceptive potential of human beings clearly appears through a broader and comprehensive approach to the dreaming process, **an approach not confined to dream interpretation. Such an approach considers that dreams are the result of an exchange process.** In fact, dreams appear to be the result of a kind of "continuous breathing" between the inner and outer worlds of individuals. When we breathe we take air in, we transform it and reject it. Through breathing we are continuously exchanging with our environment through our lungs and the entire surface of the skin. This air contains a lot of intangible things and has a lot of properties. For example, it can be warm and our skin transmits the information, "it's warm." This is a reception of information from the intangible environment. And our body emits in the air, its odors, its hormones, its energy, its emotions and its electromagnetic field. Ideas and thoughts are also emitted in the environment through the body, whether or not we use speech. We can schematically represent as follows a human being surrounded by all he/she emits in the atmosphere and which contains the energy field:

Diagram n° 3 a person in an *information sphere:*

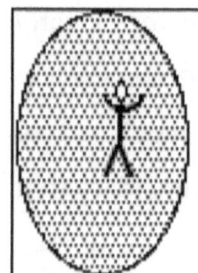

The information sphere includes any invisible information emitted by a person + invisible information from the place where the person is standing.
=
The atmosphere surrounding a person

Chinese acupuncturists already knew millennia ago the inner human energy fields. The aim of Chinese acupuncture is to allow a correct flow of energy in the body to keep it healthy or to restore good health. It is only recently, in comparison with China, that the Western world is discovering the energy aspect of the human body. Since 1875, the Western world has understood that the brain contains electric currents. And since 1929, we have been technologically able to observe the electrical emissions of the brain thanks to the electroencephalograph. This device permits doctors to amplify the electric signals that are picked up by electrodes fixed on people's skulls.[11] In 2005, Jonathan R. Wolpaw received an award from the Altran Foundation for Innovation[12] for a brain-powered remote control for totally paralyzed people. This BCI system (Brain Computer Interface) makes use of the electricity emitted by the brain, the EEG technology and sophisticated software to enable totally paralyzed people to use a computer.[13] Thanks to this system they can now write texts and send e-mails.

Many researchers are now working in this field. In 1939, Kirlian, a Russian researcher, has invented a technology that can photograph the energy field of human beings and of plants.[14] Other researchers in different countries also conducted similar researches. The Kirlian process has been used for medical diagnosis and also in agriculture. It is nowadays generally admitted that our body is surrounded by invisible emanations, and it has been made scientifically clear that all the cells of our body are constantly exchanging energy.[15] Some of these invisible emanations, like the electricity emitted by the brain, can now be used by paralyzed people to control remotely a computer. From now on we shall call these emanations surrounding every person an *information sphere or information bath*. Although we are unable to see this information sphere, we can sense it as the special ambiance of a person, the one that we perceive on the first seconds of an encounter with a person. This information sphere also contains information from the environment where the body of the person stands. This last piece of information can be constituted by emanations of some other people, the emissions of plants and of animals, also by solar or earth energy. It is always through the body that you have access to the intangible information world. We are all emitters and receivers of information. For example, when you speak, you emit sound information with your tongue. You receive sound information from the environment (mainly) with your ears. In the case of sound, this information is clear for your conscious mind, which accepts it. From that acceptance you admit the reality of sounds, even though they are invisible. The same occurs with regards to odors--we admit their existence even though we cannot touch or see them. In addition to receiving information, everyone emits information back into the environment such as: emotions, feelings, odors, noises, and thoughts.[16] Continuous breathing occurs between the information received by the body and the information it emits in exchange. But our conscious mind drastically filters this mass of information that our body is able to receive from the environment.[17] Such a drastic selection deprives us of a huge wealth of information. This filtering function of the conscious mind has been noticed in the field of medical hypnosis and also by scientists studying the functioning of the brain. Aldous Huxley[18] concluded that the brain and the nervous system act as a reducing valve:

> *Reflecting on my experience, I find myself agreeing with the eminent Cambridge philosopher, Dr C. D. Broad, 'that we should do well to consider much more seriously than we have hitherto been inclined to do the type of theory which Bergson put forward in connection with memory and sense perception. The suggestion is that the function of the brain and nervous system and sense organs is in the main eliminative and not productive. Each person is at each moment capable of remembering all that has ever happened to him and of perceiving everything that is happening everywhere in the universe. The function of the brain and nervous system is to protect us from being overwhelmed and confused by this mass of largely useless and irrelevant knowledge, by shutting out most of what we should otherwise perceive or remember at any moment, and leaving only that very small and special selection which is likely to be practically useful.*

John Locke, in *An Essay Concerning Human*

Understanding,[19] shows how much the conscious minds of the learned people of his time played this role of reducing valve, not just regarding information stemmed from the unconscious mind but from the normal rational capacities of reflection of conscious mind itself:

> The imputation of novelty is a terrible charge amongst those, who judge of men's heads, as they do of their perukes [wigs], by the fashion; and can allow none to be right, but the received doctrines. Truth scarce ever yet carried it by vote anywhere at its first appearance: new opinions are always suspected, and usually opposed, without any other reason, but because they are not already common. But truth, like gold, is not the less so, for being newly brought out of the mine.

The dream-reality work will allow you to make your conscious mind more flexible so that you will benefit from more information than what is available to the average researcher. The simple observation of dreams clearly shows that dreams are intimately connected to the waking life. Many people know from experience that the content of dreams can be directly influenced by previous daily events. For example, the characters of a movie can appear in your dreams mixed with some personal elements. Daily life concerns also appear in dreams. A human being cannot survive without a permanent exchange with its environment. **Dreaming, like the majority of physical and psychological processes, consists mainly in processes of exchange and emission/reception of information.** Some information that dreams convey to the conscious mind is clear, but the majority of dream information appears like nonsense to the conscious mind of people who have not been trained to understand their dreams. To them, the dream content appears useless, grotesque, ridiculous or threatening. As we generally do not understand the meaning of dreams, and as we do not know why dreams exist, we simply tend to forget about them. And yet scientific investigation has proved that deprived from dreams, human beings are destined for death. This function that we believe useless is actually indispensable.

Our attitude toward the dreaming brain is a fundamental mistake of our civilization, which has not been able to take profit from this natural ability to accelerate its development and the pace of scientific and technological innovation. Generally speaking, we content ourselves with taking very little from our extremely rich informational environment. A more comprehensive approach to the dream process makes it possible to understand the dream language, which in turn leads to benefiting from more environmental information. Such a use of the dream process will help you overcome the drastic limitations imposed on you by your conscious mind.[20]

There is no separation between the physical world studied by modern science and the invisible world that surrounds our body. As we have seen, the tangible and the intangible worlds are especially interwoven in human beings. Understanding better the dream process is a privileged means to understand better both the functioning of the material and intangible worlds and their synergy. Through a systematic observation of the connections that exist between your dreams and your reality, you will become more creative in all fields. The immaterial side of life was so important to ancient people that if you cannot experience what they lived, it is hardly possible to understand them properly. Observing the connections between your dreams and your reality will help you better access this intangible energy side of life that we are no longer able to consciously perceive in the waking state and, hence, ignore. At this stage of our evolution we have lost this ability and developed other faculties of the brain. However, our body is still able to perceive the energies of the cosmos, of the places where you stand, of the people you interact with, of the things you touch. It transmits all these perceptions to the brain, most of the time as dreams and intuitions. The body has its proper intelligence and the thing that matters the most to it is the preservation of its life force. The body is extremely sensitive to energy and to everything that disturbs its energy potential. This is why malfunctioning electrical devices placed near the bed beside the head of the sleeping person often gives place to horrible nightmares that will disappear once these items are removed or repaired. If you systematically observe the connections between your dreams and your reality, you will discover the mental universe of the ancient peoples who were so interested in the forces coming from the sun and other planets in the intangible links between persons and in life-energy preservation. To them, Gods were not divine entities in the meaning of modern religions, but springs of energies where they could "drink". Christiane Desroches-Noblecourt, a French Egyptologist, said about the Egyptian religion:

> This religion was not a mystic, but physics... Therefore, it is outdated to continue considering as "gods" these human figures with animal heads that cover the walls of the temples. They simply are the various expressions of the divine. Their attributes permitted to distinguish their special function in the divine machinery: they were the energies at work in the conservation of the universe.[21]

Through my experience, I have noticed that dreams act as a bridge between the conscious mind, and a much wider consciousness, from now on called the *greater consciousness*. Of course, I don't ask you to simply believe me (which would be useless) but instead to conduct your own research with the help of the methods I have developed over many years. The greater consciousness contains much more information than the conscious mind. It contains all the information that the body picks up in its environment (immediate or remote) that does not reach the conscious mind. We can schematically represent as follows the situation of people who almost "do not dream" and who do not pay attention to their dreams. These persons benefit very little from the information picked up by the body, which transmits it to the greater consciousness, which in turn conveys it in part to the conscious mind through dreams. Which can be shown as follows.

Diagram n° 4.

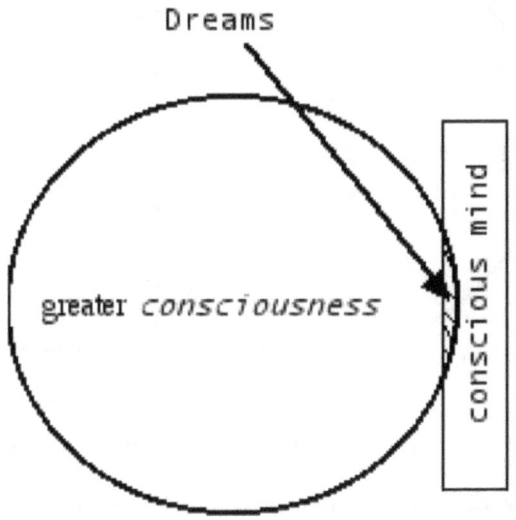

In contrast, by understanding the connections between dreams and reality, it is possible to attain the following state of development. In this state, the conscious mind has been progressively enlarged and made more flexible and the person can make better use of the information contained in the greater consciousness. In other words, the conscious mind grows by understanding the dream language.

Diagram n° 5

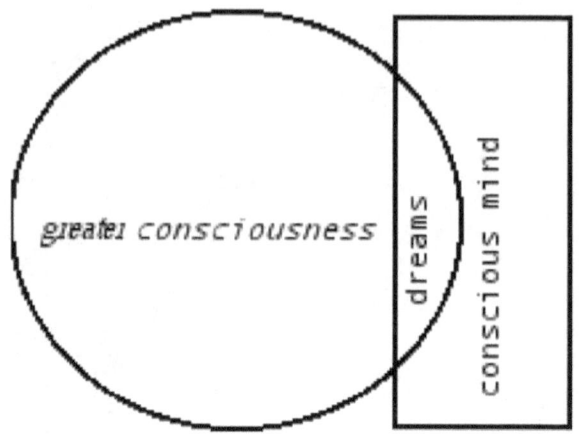

Observing the connections between dreams and reality will allow people interested in this possibility to prepare themselves naturally, safely and at their own pace to a new stage of development. When a person reaches this stage of development, she can access directly information received by the greater consciousness even while awake. Intuition is part of this phenomenon. This person will naturally access this information without the need to use special techniques. We can schematize this third stage of development as follows:

Diagram n° 6:

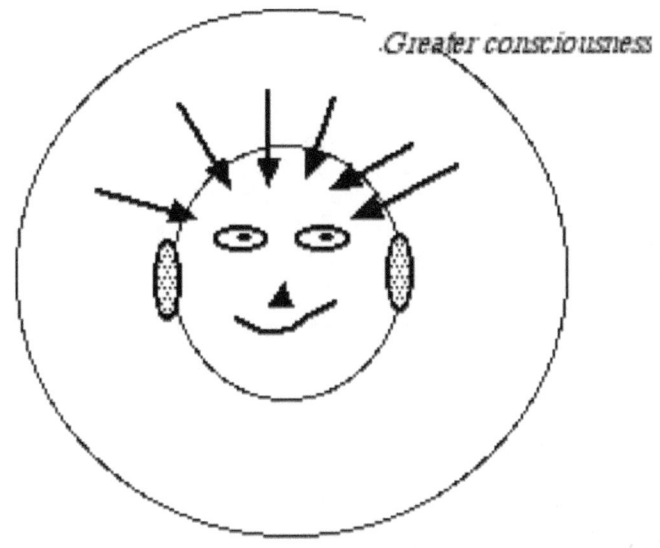

People having achieved this stage have developed capabilities that are generally considered extraordinary but which will be more common in the future when humanity is more developed. Some now-disappeared civilizations had already explored these possibilities, and traces (more or less distorted) of the knowledge they had gathered have crossed time through religions, occultism, ancient legal systems and popular belief.

The easiest way to check for yourself the reality of these possibilities is to observe the connections between your dreams and your reality. In the following chapter I will give you all the information you need to conduct your own investigation.

CHAPTER 2

An efficient method for observing the connections between your dreams and your reality

In this chapter, I am going to explain how to efficiently explore your dreaming process, so that you can better understand the way the brain functions in regard to symbolic communication. You will also be able to use your dream process to develop your creativity and to get answers to your questions in all fields of life. Through applying this method, step by step you will see how your unconscious and the ancient layers that link us to our most remote ancestors work.

1. How to observe your dreaming process

The best way to observe the dreaming process is not to focus on dreams alone. Instead, you should observe simultaneously your dreams and your reality. Write down your dreams and the main events of your waking life, and carry on simple experiments in your waking life in order to observe their consequences on the dreaming process. If it is true that reality influences dreams,[22] you will discover very soon for yourself how much your dreams shape your reality, even when you do not remember them.

Dreams may seem unimportant and to have no connection with reality. Through keeping a dream-reality journal you will gradually see the connection that exists between the dreaming process and the information world. The existence of such a connection will allow you to understand very precisely the meaning of your own and unique dream language. It will also help you become more conscious of what occurs at the energy level in your environment. The dream-reality work will show you that the greater consciousness is highly interested in the preservation of your life force and is extremely sensitive to the energetic quality of your environment and to the vitality of other people.

Each of us has his own specific dream vocabulary that was formed in the beginning of life when the conscious mind and the greater consciousness were discovering the world (through the body and its senses). This is when most of the programming of the brain in regard to the dream language occurred. I have seen, through my personal work and through helping other people in their dream-reality work, that the dream-language is stable along the life. After an average of one year of work you will have decoded most of your specific dream vocabulary. Only a few new symbols will appear from time to time in a dreamer's life. Personal work is absolutely necessary if you want to understand your own dream-information and benefit from it.

To understand your dream language, you cannot expect help from ancient or modern dream dictionaries, which pretend to give you a ready-to-use interpretation of dream symbols that would be valid for all of us. This is not true; every person has programmed his brain in a specific way in the first years of his life. It is better to avoid this kind of literature, which frequently leads to mistranslation of your unique dream vocabulary. Moreover, this literature is full of fears and superstitions passed from generation to generation. Most of the time dream dictionaries will only blur the understanding of your dreaming process. It is regrettable that dream dictionaries are the most read literature about dreams; being so inaccurate they have understandably contributed to deter many serious people from the study of dreams.

Every person has a unique dream language, this cannot be stressed enough. However one can share with some hues, some great dream symbols common to human groups or to the whole humanity. For example, for many dreamers the symbol "house" can stand for the body, the symbol "on the left" is for the intuitive aspect of the mind and the symbol "on the right" for the logical aspect. Left and right will also represent the feminine and the masculine aspects of the mind. What is "in the forefront" relates to the future for many dreamers, while what is "behind" generally relates to the past of the dreamer. Streets, highways, country roads, lanes, or mountain tracks are often varied representations of the life path, the destiny (and as I will explain later that dreams with these themes are useful to researchers, as they often show how things are going in their investigations). Most of the time you will see these symbols appear in your dreams when in the waking life you have to make some important decisions regarding your personal life or the works you are conducting.

At the beginning of your dream-reality work, you may find help by using dictionaries of symbols, which do not relate to dreams but explain the meaning of symbols throughout the ages and for different peoples.[23] Learning about the meaning of symbols is an excellent way to make your conscious mind more flexible in order to better understand your own world of symbols. Mental flexibility is what we need the most in order to understand the realities that are of our greater consciousness but that are alien to the focus of our conscious mind.

The best and easiest way I have found to discover the meaning of my dreams and to access more information on my intangible environment is by keeping a dream-reality journal. In this journal, I write down all the dreams I remember, the main lines of my reality, and the experiments I did. For example, as an experiment you can decide to sleep in special places, go on a diet, overeat, visit many people or completely isolate yourself for some time (without watching TV, listening radio or talking over the phone) while continuing to keep your dream-reality journal.[24] I have experienced all the above and other kinds of experiences, and as a result I have detected the important things to write down regarding dreams and reality.

2. How to record your dreams

It is much easier to remember your dreams when you wake up; this is therefore the best time to write them down. Some authors also advise to make note of them during the night and therefore to have everything paper and pencils ready next to the bed. It can be done, but paying so much attention to dreams can be stressful and sometimes blocking. If you want to do a long-drawn-out job, then do it in a relaxed way, sleep normally and as comfortably as possible. With practice, you will remember more and more about your dreams and you will also improve your memory in general.

If at the beginning you cannot remember your dreams, do not be discouraged. Memory of your dreams rapidly increases when you pay attention to them. At the beginning of your dream-reality work, if you cannot remember the scenery and the content of your dreams, just write down your feelings upon awakening. Observe your mood and take notes about it. Are you happy, sad, peaceful? Also take note of your physical state: are you in good physical condition, or do you feel tired? You will see that in so doing, little by little you will come to remember more and more about your dreams.

As soon as you wake up, note the thoughts wandering in your mind. At this time, if instead of thinking about your dreams, you immediately think about daily life concerns, your chances of remembering your dreams will decrease. On a practical ground, if you are very tired and sleep only enough for physical recovery, you will decrease the possibility of remembering your dreams and you will decrease the quality of your dreams. An easy technique you can use to help remember your dreams is to tell yourself before you fall asleep: "I want to dream and I want to remember my dreams". This is very simple but effective.[25]

At the beginning of your dream-reality work, the fundamental attitude you should adopt is neutrality. You should observe your dream-process as if you were a movie camera; write down everything you remember without any judgment, without filtering, without omitting what you dislike. When you write down your dreams do not try to understand them. Just write and let all your emotions, feelings and ideas emerge. Simply write down all you remember, and above all avoid complex analysis of dream messages. In this regard, the less you know about popular dream knowledge the better it will be to do fruitful work. In time, you will be able to understand precisely and rationally your own dream symbols (I will tell you why later on.) You will also notice that some dreams are crystal-clear and do not need to be interpreted through a psychoanalytical approach or another method.

A second fundamental attitude is the courage to write down everything you remember even if these memories are painful, shameful, scary or disturbing. Again, be neutral and tolerant like a movie-camera. Write down all you can remember. **All the dreams you can remember must be written down without selecting the ones you believe to be important**. Every dream is important if you want to understand the connections between your dreams and your reality. For example, a short and simple dream like "I dreamed that some beautiful shoes were on sale at the butchers" contains valuable information.

Also do not be afraid to take note of things regarding death or death itself. Most of the time death in dreams announces a big change in your life or personality or a rebirth. It may also show you that you need to completely change the way you are conducting a piece of research. Why being afraid of dreams announcing death? Why not pay attention to them, as they can also be warning dreams that can save your life? There are many cases of dreams relating to actual deaths. The event is announced in the dreaming state through specific dreams.[26] It seems logical that by the end of our lives, the body sends to the brain information about the fact that it is dying, creating specific dreams (that I have not yet personally experienced).

Having spoken of the hard subject of death, let us now speak about life. In the dreaming state, regardless of sex and age, everybody can give birth or be pregnant. It is no longer the women's privilege. Most of the time dreams about being pregnant and giving birth are related to creativity. Therefore, this dream theme and everything in dreams that is related to new life, birth, growing or blooming plants is of paramount importance for researchers and inventors. When these themes appear in the course of a research work you know you are on the right path. As for explicit sexual dreams, I have seen through my dream-reality work that they can simply portray an exchange of information between people. Many sexual dreams convey a non-sexual message and you should not hesitate to note each detail of them without any shame to your conscious mind. Sometimes you may dream you have an intercourse with a researcher of your team, and you will see from your dream-reality journal that the day before you had a meeting with this person where an intense exchange of information took place. So your dream-sex simply showed how much you were "connected" with this person during the meeting.

Let us take a different example: dreaming about an interrupted intercourse does not necessarily mean that this will happen in reality or that it is a sexual message. It can mean a sudden, unexpected and unpleasant end of a relationship with a relative or the imposed end of an investigation you were conducting. As for bananas, doors, staircases, birds and other symbols that Freud considered to be sexual symbols, one should update ones ideas. Sexuality has become freer than during Freud's time, and consequently dreams and reality have changed a lot. Also, our conscious mind is less strict regarding this natural aspect of life. You will notice through your own dream-reality work that your body has its own "dreams" that it uses to satisfy some of its needs and also to send information to the brain about what is not working properly in the body. Such information is available to the conscious mind through dreams long before we feel bodily discomfort in our waking state.

In short, we should take note of all the dreams in the way they speak to our memory and describe the dream characters and the stage of the dream in a manner as accurate and detailed as possible. For example, if you dream of a cat, you should take note of its color, its size, its spatial position in comparison with yours or with the spatial position of other dream characters (to the left, to the right, behind, in front of, in the middle, etc.). You should also take note of everything you perceive about this cat. Take note of the appearance of its fur, and of its eyes. Look at both eyes--are they similar in color? In shape? In their expression? Is it a female or a male cat? From experience, I know that in *my* dream language (though perhaps not yours), cats represent the true face of the people around me and also my own. I know that a cat with an unhealthy fur is related to a person having little vitality, in other words a low level of life force. It is of paramount importance to write down all your feelings, even when they seem unrelated with the main topic of the dream. For example, in a dream you can laugh at something that would be horrible in the waking life and on the contrary you can feel a lot of pain for something that would be insignificant in the waking state. You should write down all your feelings: joy, pain, love, hatred, fear, anger, anxiety, sadness, etc. Also take note of all your physical sensations like cold, heat, paralysis, lightness, quickness, and slowness. If you hear some music in your dream describe it, take note of the content of songs, take also note of the tales you hear, of the characters. You will see that more communication generally occurs in the dreaming state than in reality. In dreams everything is able to speak, from stones to plants and animals. They can speak your own language.

Sometimes, you or other characters can speak some language you do not speak in the waking state. In my dreams, I notice that when there is a repetition of the same words, sentences or images, this is important information. Sometimes I dream of some foreign words whose meaning I do not know, and I find it amusing and often instructive to check, when possible, their meaning in a dictionary upon awakening. When I was living in New York, at the limit of Little Italy and China Town, many times I dreamed in Chinese, a language I don't speak but the dominant language of my close environment.

It is also important to take note of your special position when you appear as one of your dream characters. Are you in the center, to the right, to the left, in front of or behind someone, something or a place? Are you standing on the ground, on water or in the sky? You should write down all you remember. For example, all the details of clothes: color, composition and shape are a great source of valuable dream information. Take note of all your physical sensations and discomforts: toothaches, earaches, lightness or difficulty of movement, for example, because you are carrying a heavy load. You should describe with as much detail as possible everything you carry in the dream state. If it is a luggage, write about its shape, color, weight, easiness or difficulty to carry it, if there are rollers or even wings on your luggage. Do you like your luggage? Did somebody help you carry it, or did you decide to abandon it because you were carrying useless things, or carrying nothing at all? With which hand did you hold your luggage: right or left hand? Is your luggage in front of you or behind you? Did you push your luggage with difficulty, or was it following you easily? For example, a researcher who dreams many times that he is carrying too much heavy luggage should better clarify his thinking, forget about some theories and beliefs which are killing his creativity.

If you dream about a house (or other kinds of homes), do

not hesitate to take note of all the details of this house, even if it takes a long time. The time spent will be greatly rewarded. Describe all the rooms you enter and particularly cellars, attics, kitchens and bathrooms. In houses, everything is interesting and informative. From my own experience, I know that the houses of my dreams (when there are not real houses that I see in the dream state) usually give me accurate information about my health. And I could notice, like doctors in antiquity already did it,[27] that physical disorders appear in dreams long before they manifest themselves in reality. Because of this, it is very interesting to get to the meaning of your dreams in order to take preventive action as soon as possible. I can observe that water leaks in dreams are connected with energy loss and fatigue in the waking life. If no preventive measures are taken they may lead to depression.

The state of dream attics and roofs portray very often what is occurring in your physical brain and also in your mind. For example a messy dream attic will show a researcher that his mind is confused and that he should better clarify his thinking if he wishes to achieve some results. In other words the way he thinks is too messy. I personally love the cellars in my dream houses because it is related to my physical and psychological heritage. It is also a place that has inspired me for my works on ancient Rome and ancient Egypt. For many dreamers, the cellar of the dream house is like the dreamers' roots. One can get their information about the past of humanity and about his specific family past: his biological and psychological heredity.

The dream-reality work will teach you a lot about nature. The greater consciousness is much more linked to nature than our conscious mind. In many dreams the greater consciousness will make use of images portraying natural phenomena like growth, sprouting, decay and fading of plants, earthquakes, and tidal waves. For example, if you have been investigating for a while without achieving any result and you dream that a strong wind is pushing you, you may expect an acceleration of your present work-- things will soon move as if pushed by the wind. Nature in dreams gives place to symbols that are common to many people in the world. It appears through stars, moon, sun, the sea, light, shade, obscurity, wind, cold, heat and mostly water. Water in dreams plays an important role, as important as the role it plays in our waking life and in our body. Water changed into ice in your dreams will carry specific information. For example, if you are working with another person and you and this person have agreed to share all information about the investigation, a dream showing you this person in a block of ice informs you that you should not rely on her for sharing information. Cold, snow and ice in dreams often portray difficulties to survive, decreasing life force, and selfishness--though they may have a totally different meaning for people living in the North Pole. You will learn through your own dream-reality work what it specifically means to you. The way water looks in dreams (crystal clear, muddy, colored) may transmit information about people around you and also about yourself.

In dreams, plants in many cases are surprising representations of peoples' state of mind or bodily condition. For example you may see in a dream a plant that grows very quickly and invades all the space in your living room. Some plants that have big apparent roots but no earth may appear to people who are immigrants in waking life. In dreams there are also withered plants, plants full of flowers or fruits. Some plants may ask you water or more space, while some others will warn you that you water them too much or they will ask you for pure spring water instead of tap water. Water is extremely important in dreams, whether it is a glass of water, bottle of water, pot of water, bath, shower, river, lake, ocean, rain, swimming pool, wells or puddles.

The simultaneous observation of your dreams and your reality will be useful to learn what aspects of your realities are meant by the different kinds of water in your dreams. For example, through my dream-reality work, I could learn that the sea, due to it immensity, represents the unlimited information wealth of my greater consciousness and also the collective consciousness of humankind. Swimming pools, on the other hand, usually portray my conscious mind with its limitations. Symbolically, if your dreams take you to the sea you will have many more opportunities to achieve discoveries in your fields than with dreams that take you to a swimming pool. In order to find new avenues and new archaeological sites, let us follow the road that dreams often point you to.

Our body is a sophisticated detection tool. It is much more efficient than the nuclear magnetic resonance magnetometers used with great success by the archaeologist Franck Goddio, but which supposes the preliminary knowledge thanks to historical testimonials of the approximate sites to search. It is interesting to quote Franck Goddio when he speaks about the technology he used to search the site of the Bay of Aboukir:

> *If you dive in the harbor without prior knowledge you'll find nothing, see nothing. You must do very sophisticated electronic prospecting and gather very complex data in order to know where to dig.*[28]

Our body is much cleverer than all sophisticated modern technology to sense the vibes emitted by objects, animals, and people. In order to benefit from this natural ability of the body, we must learn how to use it better and we must develop better communication between our conscious and unconscious minds. Developing this ability of detection has a big advantage over using technology alone, as our unconscious does not need historical data to find archeological sites that are of interest to us. The unconscious will be attracted to some places according to the laws of the intangible world: affinity, resonance, and attraction between the researcher and the objects he is seeking. For now, as researchers having not yet developed these abilities, we can thank the available technology. It is much better than nothing. And yet, the technologies we admire so much are only crutches compared to the possibilities of the body. Fortunately, intuitive archeologists have ever existed. Most of the time, they did not remember their dreams, but they followed their intuition and found "by coincidence" important archeological remains. But when you begin exploring the connections between your dream and your reality, you will see that no "coincidence" took place in these events. The truth is that the body of the researchers had detected information and sent it to the conscious brain as intuition, attraction, and impulse. I found a striking example of this process in the DVD of Franck Goddio's exhibition about the sunken treasures of Ancient Egypt. Here is the dialogue between French archaeologist Franck Goddio and the diver Jean-Claude Roubaud coming back into the boat after having dived in search for archeological artifacts:

Franck Goddio: "Did you see anything?"

> *Jean-Claude Roubaud: "Hard to say, but I have a feeling something's there... I think I have it, I'll say maybe... maybe it's not true, but I.... Sometimes I think: 'Ah, it's strange, I like this place' and then I find something.*

It is often through emotion, attraction, repulsion that the conscious and the unconscious work together in the waking state. This man obviously makes use of the information of his unconscious when he dives in search of old artifacts. With the dream-reality method, he would considerable increase his natural ability to communicate with his unconscious so that he takes the right route in archeological sites. I close here this parenthesis and I come back to the study of the dream process and to the dream theme of "roads".

In our world, where instability is a condition lived by many people in their private and professional life, dreams portraying the dreamer on the road are abundant. The road followed by the dreamer may be a jammed highway, a silent avenue in an empty city, a beautiful path along a river, a street covered with a bright white snow. The dreamer may sometimes indefinitely turn at a roundabout or hesitate on the way to follow at a crossroads. He may also have to clear a way through the undergrowth or fight obstacles.

Sometimes the dreamer knows where he is going; sometimes he walks in total obscurity until someone helpful comes and lights the way with a powerful flashlight.

If we pay attention to dreams portraying the dreamer (and other people) on the road, we can get a lot of information about our destiny and the way to achieve results in investigations. Dreams of "roads" often show researchers the path they should follow to find what they are seeking. Sometimes they even show what they are not yet searching for! But as they are not aware of their importance and meaning, researchers ignore these useful dreams and continue to search blindly with their conscious mind alone. Here is a beautiful example of a dream made by a person whose researches were successful.

I dream I am on a road where there are cars, trucks, buses. I am the only person riding a bike but I pass all the other vehicles on this road. Sometimes I am on the right of the road, sometime on the left and sometimes in the middle. My route

> *is not straight and I can observe it from the skies as a thin copper thread that unfolds with my progress on the road. Suddenly, I become a big plane and I take off. I can hear the other people on the road thinking 'He took the road for a takeoff strip'.*

Information on the way to achieving fruitful research may also be transmitted by other kinds of dreams. For example Descartes, who despite his rational mind paid attention to his dreams, had the following dream when he was writing *Discourse of the Method*. This dream was reported by Baillet as "Descartes' dreams of November 10, 1619."[29]

> *A short time later, he had a third dream. He dreamt that he found a book on his table without knowing where it came from. He opened it and as he realized that it was a dictionary he became very pleased and thought that this book should be very useful. At the same time he found another book in his hands, which was also completely new and he did not know where it came from, either. He saw that this book was a book of poetry from several authors, entitled "corpus poëtarum" etc.. He felt very interested in reading something in this book, opened it and fell on the following line: "quod vitae sectabor iter?" (Which way shall I follow in my life?).*

The other reported dreams gave some guidance to

Descartes. Notably, they pointed out a strong imbalance between the right and the left sides of his dream-body. As René Descartes never kept a dream-reality diary, we have not enough dream-reality material about him and we cannot accurately know in which field of his waking life he was so imbalanced, if this was a temporary or permanent imbalance, or if this dream conveyed information regarding not himself but another person from whom information was unconsciously picked up during the day.

If you want to benefit from the information conveyed by dreams showing you on the road, it is important to write down everything you remember and to describe as well as possible everything you can see or feel. If, for example you are in a car, you should note its color, the location of the steering wheel (at the right or at the left or other unusual location), who is driving, how, at night or during the day? If it is at night is there light on the road? How do you feel? Happy? Stressed? Confident? What do you sense in your body: Comfort? Discomfort? These kinds of dreams are important for researchers and they should learn to make use of them in order to avoid spending many years on useless roads. Moreover, this theme of dreams is one of the easiest to understand.

In summary, when taking note of your dreams, it is essential to note all you remember about your dreams and to note all your dreams without selecting only the ones your conscious mind finds worth writing down. In the beginning it is better not to try to understand the meaning of your dreams. Instead, focus your attention on writing down all you can about your dreams and be as neutral as possible. Understanding the meaning of your dreams is interesting, but there is a greater benefit a researcher will draw from the dream-reality: a better communication between his conscious and his unconscious mind, or if you prefer a better synergy between the right and left hemispheres of the brain. As for the "translation" of your dream language, it will be much easier to achieve after some time, because you will see that the same dream symbols and dream themes will appear in simultaneity with a same event having taken place in your waking life. This repetition of waking life events and concomitant dream events will allow an accurate deciphering of your dream language. For example, if whenever you have met a lawyer in your waking life you have dreamt the night before or the night after the encounter that you have met or you were going to meet a mathematician, you will know that in your symbolic dream language mathematics stands for law.

In the beginning of my work I read everything I could find about dreams and of course the works of Jung and Freud and other specialists. Initially I tried to interpret my dreams according to the psychoanalytical theories and soon I realized that most of the time these theories were misleading me and preventing me from learning the best of the information conveyed by my dreams. Later on, the meaning of almost all my dreams was made naturally clear through a comparison between events taking place in my waking life and the dreams I had. In other words, after some time it is easy when you read back your journal to note that a certain kind of dream appears in connection to a certain kind of real life event.

However, psychoanalysis may be useful to understand better some of your dreams related to psychological conflicts. In time you will learn through your dream-reality work which dreams are "psychological dreams" that can benefit from the works of these specialists. All of us have unresolved psychological problems, this is life. Dreams are an opportunity to work on these problems often rejected by the conscious mind and to free the energy they have locked in you. I have observed that the most important psychological dreams appear when they are reactivated by a waking life event, but also when I have the energy and the peace of mind to work them. This is why they generally happen when one makes a retreat, and this even if no external events reactivate them. In such a case I feel that the energy I do not use for outer life is used for inner repairing. The more psychological problems you can solve, the more your dream capabilities will be available for other tasks. After 20 years of work on my dreams, a small portion of them--that I am now able to distinguish easily from the other kinds of dreams--require a psychological approach, whereas, the wide majority of my dreams are understandable more accurately through the simultaneous observation of dream and reality over a long period of time. Therefore be patient, take note of every dream and also observe your reality. Thanks to the understanding of your dream information you will save time by avoiding mistakes, pitfalls and dead ends in your researches and in your waking life. You will get a considerable advantage on all other researchers ignoring the dream-reality method.

3. Notes you should take about your waking life

Notes about your waking life do not need to be as detailed as notes about your dreams. My long work on the issue will save you time, as I have learned the useful things to note about the waking life. Regarding the waking life, you only need to outline the main events of the day. Some observations are very important in order to understand the way you pick up information from your environment. For example, it is useful to note the places where you have been during the day, the places where you have slept, and above all the people you have met. Regarding these people, just write down the main subject of your conversation and the circumstances of your encounter, whether planned meeting or mere coincidence. It is also important to note your feelings (joy, sadness, indifference, boredom, anxiety) or body feelings (well-being, fatigue, nervousness, muscular tensions) and to note the location where the meeting took place. Locations are very important elements, insofar as every place is full of intangible information that your body will pick up when you stand in a place.[30] This aspect is very important for archaeologists. Before restoring old artifacts that had just been found, archeologists should better sleep beside them when they are still strongly charged with the information bath from which they have been taken. In so doing, they would give themselves more opportunities to unconsciously pick up information about the people who, a long time ago, had used and made these objects. Once restored, touched by many people, and watched by crowds of curious visitors in museums, these objects have lost most of their original information and have been charged with new information from the modern world. I have also observed that water tends to eliminate information from objects. I was impatient to visit Franck Goddio's exhibition in Paris in order to experience what my body would pick up from remains that had stayed so long under the sea. During my visit to the exhibition I could put my hands on a naos (a small stone temple) - our hands are powerful information sensors. The following night I had only a strong dream in which I attended the mating of a black bull and a white cow taking place in a beautiful green lawn in front of a building that seemed to be their home. These animals were impressive by their high energy and their gigantic bodies. The energy potential of the naos must have been extremely high to have survived despite this long under-water stay and the archeological repairs and handling for the exhibition. Modern man believes he is only looking at old stones, coins, jewels, and statues when he visits museums. But his body "sees" the whole information and energy of these objects. And to our greater consciousness this is what matters the most, this is what it wants to tell us through our dreams that we no longer understand and "listen". I found the following in the writing of Eunapius, about the destruction of Canopus' ancient temples by the Christians: "These people, all together had the zeal of quarrymen to destroy our sanctuaries as if they were only dealing with stones..."

The temples and statues of ancient Egypt were much more than the objects we now only perceive. They were strongly charged with information and energy thanks to techniques we ignore.

It is easy to sense the informational aspect of places, which we commonly call ambiance. Everybody has already sensed how different are the atmospheres of churches, pubs, libraries, gardens, or beaches. It is also easy to perceive the difference in atmosphere between your home and other people's homes. The atmosphere we are speaking of is not the one created by the interior design but by the intangible information contained in the house. In fact we are able to sense the energies of premises and other places where we stand. In the waking state, some people have poor consciousness of these energies, while others are highly sensitive to them. (Animals are extremely sensitive to the energy of places.) But even though one cannot consciously perceive the intangible energy of a place, one's greater consciousness always stores all the intangible information that is available there. Dreams will allow a person, who in the waking state is insensitive to this dimension of life, to get valuable information about the intangible quality of the places where she lives or works. Taking advantage of the dream-reality work will counter-balance the lack of conscious perception of the various information baths surrounding us.

In order to draw the maximum benefits from your dream-reality work, here are summarized the most important things to note:

-All the main events of your waking life: daily activities, trips, parties, moving, big decisions you make, and important achievements.

-People engaged in creative tasks and in scientific research should also note the different stages of their work and the way they live their creativity or investigation (for example: the days when they feel happy and satisfied, and the days when they hesitate, feel discontent and uninspired).

- The people you have met.

- The places where you have been, visits to friends or family homes, visit to different laboratories, places where your daily activities took place.

If you would like to use your dreams to improve your physical and mental health and to detect future health problems,[31] it is important to take note of all that regards your health in waking life, even the slight discomforts you have suffered. You can for example take note of a cold, a flu, muscular tensions, good or bad physical condition. If you are an athlete take note of how your training progresses. Regarding mental health: take note of your good or bad moods when you wake up, during the day, after meetings or when you go to unusual places.

All this information is very useful. Time and patience are required, but the results are worthwhile. Thanks to this preliminary work you will be able to use a powerful technique to get answers to your questions in any field. Before explaining this technique, I am going to present the many results we can achieve after one year of dream reality work. Even some of my students who had no intuition and no memory of their dreams at the beginning of the work achieved these results.

CHAPTER 3

The world you will discover through the dream reality work

I have been exploring the dream-reality connections for a long time and experienced the influences from places, people, food, homeopathic remedies, plants and many other variables on the dream process. It is also known that ancient peoples and modern traditional people have used some plants to provoke special dreams. Dream-reality work will allow achieving more results without drugs. While drugs decrease your vitality, dream-reality work increases it and contributes to your good health. Through my long dream-reality work, and through helping other people in their work, I have discovered lots of things in many fields. I will communicate here only the information that will help researchers achieve more discoveries (More results regarding other fields like health and communication can be found in my book: *The Intelligence of Dreams*.[32]), though everyone can use the method I propose for one's own aim and according to one's own interests.

As a lawyer, I was particularly interested in observing the invisible net of links between people, the energy of groups and the way people exchange energy. In the modern world, I am an unusual lawyer. And yet in ancient civilizations, lawyers did much more than know the law and apply it. They were more interested in Justice than in Law, and Justice itself was linked to the natural laws of the universe. In brief, the first priest-lawyers were truly interested in balancing the intangible relationships between human beings in order to maintain the harmony of the community.

I have sought through my investigation on the dreaming process to better understand the intangible exchanges between people. Here are some of the results that anyone can achieve after one year of studying the dream-reality connections. Even people who are less intuitive and less sensitive to their invisible environment will achieve these results. More sensitive persons may achieve the same results much faster. If you have never explored your dream process you are perfectly right to be skeptical. But please perform your own dream-reality work, this will allow you to check everything for yourself.

1. Exchanges between peoples' brains are intense in the dream state

In the dreaming state you will see that you have a collective and a personal life the same way you have them in the waking state. This means that most of the time we do not dream alone but in connection with other people. Observing the connections between dreams and reality proves that there exists a net of intangible exchanges between people. The author Robert Moss also noticed the existence of this net and named it the "psychic Internet." This "psychic Internet" connects all of us without need for computers, cell phones, TV, or even voice. In this psychic Internet all the greater consciousnesses of all the human beings communicate intensively day and night, and most of the time the conscious mind is not aware of this communication.

2. Interactions with other persons and with the environment involve intangible exchanges of energy and information

As I have already explained, everyone emits all types of information through the body and receives information from other people and places. Everyone is surrounded by his/her own unique ambiance that we call the information sphere. In this information sphere, the information we emit is mixed with the information we receive from the people around us or from the place where we are located. This can be schematized as follows:

Diagram n° 7

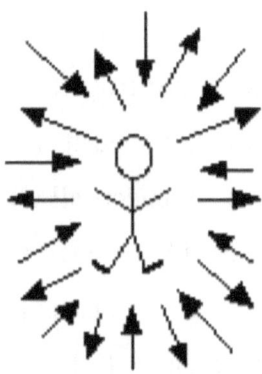

When you stand beside another person, your information sphere mixes with the information sphere of the other person. For this reason, your body picks up much more information on people than your conscious mind. What occurs when two people meet can be represented as follows.

Diagram n° 8:

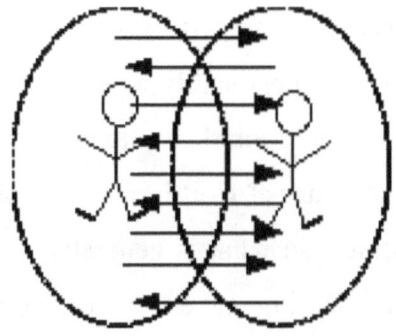

3. The greater consciousness stores information that is picked up by the body (but ignored by the conscious mind). Part of this information will nevertheless pass to the conscious mind through the canal of dreams.

When two people meet, a deep exchange occurs between their information spheres. While the conscious mind receives direct information like speech, odors, visual information, the body picks up all the intangible messages that emanate from the person and the place of the meeting. The body is able to pick up intangible information like feelings, thoughts, the physical and mental health of the other person and also information about where this person lives, his/her family context, his/her her background and so on...

The greater consciousness performs a full scanning of the health condition and personality of each person we meet. While the conscious mind is limited to information conveyed by the material world, our body picks up much more information than what is generally available to our conscious mind. During an encounter, you will benefit from all the information that is consciously picked up and also from information that is picked up by the greater consciousness and transmitted to the conscious mind through intuition and gut feelings. All the information picked up by the body reaches the greater consciousness, but in the waking state only a tiny portion of this information reaches the conscious mind. However, a bigger portion of this information can reach the conscious mind through dreams. The only inconvenience is that this information is often distorted and needs to be decoded by the conscious mind in order to be useful.

4. Dreams allow us to get more information on our environment than is generally available to the conscious mind alone.

While the conscious mind likes to filter and reject much information, the body seems eager to pick up as much information as possible from the environment. In order to become aware of the different information baths from different places and people, you may conduct the following simple and informative experiment. After having observed the dream-reality connections for some time, isolate yourself totally for a few days[33]--no contact with other people, no phone, no TV, etc.). (Depressed persons should not conduct the experiment of isolation.) Isolation allows for "cleaning" of your own information sphere from the usual emission coming from the people you live with (family or coworkers). After the isolation period, you will sense much better the difference between your proper information sphere and other people's. You will become more sensitive to the information baths of people, animals and places. I have done this experiment many times. Sometimes I have added a diet and/or homeopathic remedies that are deemed to clean the body or the mind. This practice was known as "dream incubation," which was practiced in temples in many places in ancient worlds. So doing, I could better perceive the reality of intangible psychic life that surrounds and permeates us all.

5. Some dreams cannot be explained in regard to the dreamer because they simply are environmental information picked up by the dreamer

Through my long dream-reality work, I realize that some dreams cannot be explained in regard to the dreamer because they simply are information that he has picked up from his environment or from other people. For example, when traveling, most of the time, dreams that occur to you in your hotel have no connection to your waking life. You have simply picked up information from other travelers having slept in this room before you. In such a case, it is useless to try to apply to these dreams the method of dream-interpretation or dream-direction invented by some specialists. In the same line, going to sleep to a different place is sometimes the most efficient way to get rid of some nightmares provoked by the disturbing energy fields and information of some bedrooms.

6. The body is highly sensitive to disturbing energy fields and this provokes many nightmares

Although the majority of human beings do not pay attention the "psychic pollution," this pollution exists and affects them at many levels. In some places, bad energy may create discomforts and adverse health conditions that cannot be rationally explained. It is not pure coincidence that certain places inspire artists, and maybe one day we will be able to measure the energy of places and of people.

The dream-reality work is very useful for people who have no conscious sensitivity to their environmental energy. Thanks to the information conveyed by their dreams they will be better aware of energy that may affect their physical or mental health and their creativity. The dream-reality work increases the conscious sensitivity to energy fields of places, people and objects.

7. Sleeping brains are able to communicate "wireless" at a long distance

When you are sufficiently trained, you will also experience communication at a distance during the waking state. Yes, I stress "during the waking state" because in the dream state communication at a distance is extremely common. When we sleep we all are in a deep energy exchange process, and we communicate with each other and our environment without a need for technological communication devices. It is common that researchers use this facility to communicate with their colleagues but forget completely about it when they are awake. My long work on the dream-reality connection taught me that the body picks up from a distance and in our immediate environment everything that is of interest to us or is energetically connected to us. This is enough to account for the fact that an archaeologist will dig where he feels irresistibly attracted without knowing why, instead of digging somewhere else. I have also noticed that distant communication in the dream state (and also in the waking state) occurs more frequently when there exists a strong emotional link or a strong intellectual interest between people.

8. The greater consciousness is not submitted to the same laws as the conscious mind. It is more powerful and it is freer from space-time limitations and from the cultural background of dreamers

You will soon see that the dream-reality work makes your conscious mind more flexible and open. Our greater consciousness obeys its own laws. It has its specific way to deal with "statistics," its own way to consider space and time. It is necessary to have a more opened conscious mind to accept the greater consciousness if we want to benefit from its unlimited informational wealth. In the interest of scientific research, we should pay closer attention to our greater consciousness, which is more innovative and more clever in anticipating the future. This powerful ability of the greater consciousness would be very useful to researchers.

During the waking state, We frequently use the possibilities of our limited conscious mind to project ourselves in the future or in the past. However, our greater consciousness is more clever than our conscious mind to anticipate our future or to recover information from our past for the simple reason that *much more information is available* to it and that usually this information is true. For the greater consciousness time and space *do* exist, but they do not follow the same rules. In this regard, it is hard to distinguish neatly what belongs to the intangible realm of dreams and what comes from the physical environment where a person is dreaming. For the greater consciousness, the way we consider time and space in the waking life is in many aspects wrong and useless. The way the greater consciousness deals with the space-time issue is not easy to explain, but I'll attempt to do so.

9. The *greater consciousness* is free from the limits of space

Our dreams are strongly permeated with the information that is around us in the places we have been during the day and where we are dreaming. However, you will see that sometimes your dreams also contain information that originates from extremely remote places. Our bodies are clever at picking thoughts emitted by people that may be in a different country, for example. In this case, the law of space that we use in the waking life is no longer valid. It is replaced by other laws that deal more with emotion, energy level of people and thoughts, and laws of attraction/repulsion based on energy. In other words, when you pick up information from other people in a remote place, these people are actually very close to you. This nearness may be emotional, energetic or simply the person has thought strongly about you and your body has picked up this thought from a distance. Through the dream-reality work you will notice that the thought (especially when strong emotion is added to it) seems to travel faster than light.

Many writers have already confirmed this fact. For example, in her biography the writer Nina Berberova asserts that she could see in a dream the circumstances of the death of her parents who were far away from her.[34] Our body is able to perceive from a distance events that are happening far away and that have a connection to us, and dreams convey to our conscious mind a portion of that information. Dreams allow us to free ourselves from the limits of physical space and provide a better access to the future and to the past.

10. We all shape more accurately our future in the dream state than in the waking state; during sleep we have a much wider memory

The concept of time in the dream state: accessing information from the past and anticipating the future during the dream process

Here again it is difficult to distinguish between dreamtime and the real time because in dreams they are often intermingled. Through your dream-reality work you will see that your dreams contain information on your very present life, on your near or remote past and on your future. I have tried to understand why this occurs.

First, it is easier to have your conscious mind admit the fact that some dreams contain information about the past than to admit the same about your future.

The past in your dreams:
You will see through your dream-reality work that some

dreams contain information about past events that you could not consciously be aware of. For example, an event took place, and two weeks later you know about it through a dream. In this case, your greater consciousness must have picked up the information about the event when this event occurred, but the information could not reach the conscious mind until two weeks later.

You will also notice that in the dream state you can access information about your ancestors, even your remote ones. Maybe the information is simply stored in our body cells, which may contain information from all the people who have contributed to your coming to life. What psychologists have named the transgenerational memory may simply be stored in our physical body. The dream-reality work shows that heredity is not physical alone but also psychological.

Through the dream-reality work, you will also see that you can access a *collective memory*. Accessing this wider database, you will be able to pick up information that is sometimes not available in the media industry or that is censored by the political or academic establishments. In the intangible world, nobody can block the information flow. There are no reporters to decide which information will be published, and no political powers that can bar you from knowing what you want to know. The sole censor is your own conscious mind. It is up to you to access the information you want. Carl Gustav Jung named this collective memory the "collective unconscious." Many spiritual traditions have claimed the existence of a natural collective memory called the Akashic memory or Akashic records.[35] According to these spiritual traditions, some people can access consciously or in the dream state the Akashic records. In the ancient Egyptians' *Book of the Dead*, the memory of the world is symbolized by the god Thoth taking notes while he stands beside the scales of justice.[36]

Even though the scientific community rejects this possibility that cannot be evidenced, technological progress makes now more and more plausible the existence of this kind of memory. Aren't we able to store more and more information in tinier and tinier devices? Aren't our bodies powerful receivers and emitters of information and energy? And after all, isn't memory everywhere where there is life?

So it is easier to explain why we can access information about the past during the dream process. As for information about the future, you may be more skeptical, but you will see that it is also easy to rationally explain such a phenomenon.

The future in your dreams:
Since our conscious mind is subjected to the space-time rules of the tangible world, it is much more difficult to admit the possibility of anticipating the future through dreams. Knowing the future seems impossible, unbelievable, paranormal or miraculous. But you can see for yourself, as some people already have, that dreaming your future is something very common and trivial.[37] Indeed, every night we have premonitory dreams. It is usually believed that the conscious mind plays the most important role in our lives and that the waking life is the most important part of our lives. The dream-reality work clearly shows that we are wrong. The most important things in our individual and collective lives occur during the dreamtime. It is during the dreamtime that the most

intense communication between people takes place. Every night in the brains of human beings the events of the next day (and also some important events in a remote future) are being programmed individually and collectively. The study of the connections between dreams and reality shows that in the waking life we act out individually and collectively what was programmed in our brains during the dream state. This programming is active even when we have completely forgotten our dreams. Even the persons the most closed to their inner world live widely under the programming of their brain that occurs at night during the dream process.

Other persons, more open to their inner lives, take better advantage of this phenomenon and are sometimes able to sense consciously their future. Given the fact that some information about the future reaches the conscious mind through crystal clear dreams, humanity has always known that dreams can "foretell" the future. This faculty was of high value to ancient peoples, though they believed that premonitory dreams were sent by their gods and they waited for the divine manifestation of premonitory dreams.[38] Nowadays, premonitory dreams are still considered by most of us as weird, paranormal or extraordinary. Many scientists who have never worked on their dreams simply deny the possibility of premonitory dreams. Ironic, when it would be of the greatest benefit to scientific research to use the capacity of the dreaming brain to anticipate the future. But who would tell a scientific colleague that he had a premonitory dream?

Why should the sleeping brain be denied the ability to anticipate your future when this is a natural common ability of the brain when you are awake? Everybody in the waking state naturally uses this ability. In the dream state this same ability is considerably amplified, and once you understand the dream language you will see that it is much more accurate.

Ancient and modern literature is rich in testimonials about premonitory dreams that came true.[39] How can we explain the existence of this natural ability to anticipate the future in the dream state? We can explain this phenomenon through comparing it to what occurs in the waking life. In the waking life, nobody is surprised when you tell that say next Friday by 5 pm you will meet Paul and Mary at the beach, for the simple reason that you have decided with them to meet at this place and at this time. The greater consciousness does exactly the same, but as it can access much more information than what is available to the limited conscious mind, and as it communicates more easily with other people, it can organize with more details and accuracy the next or remote future.

When you have sufficiently investigated your own dream-reality connections and decoded the majority of your dream symbols, you will notice that some events have been announced in your dreams--sometime clearly--a long time before. I have noticed in my work that some important events of my life were clearly programmed in my dreams 10 years before they occurred in my waking life. But most of the time usual events of my life are programmed the night before they will take place. The dream-reality work shows clearly that dreams are constantly shaping and preparing the waking life. But few of us are aware of this fact. When one does not understand one's dreams, one can be aware of precognitive dreams only when these dreams are crystal clear, which seldom occurs to the persons who do not pay attention to their dreams. Many people miss all their precognitive dreams because they don't understand their own dream language. They believe precognitive dreams do not exist. Some are lucky enough to benefit from occasional crystal-clear precognitive dreams. If you learn to decode your dream language thanks to the dream-reality work, you will get an incredible advantage over other researchers investigating in the same fields with their limited conscious mind alone. This will help you seize opportunities, make better decisions, overcome obstacles, and take the right direction.

In order to use the dreaming process to anticipate the future, you must learn to distinguish precognitive dreams from other dreams like desire fulfilling, dreams that result from the "digestion" of information received by the conscious mind, psychological dreams, and recurring nightmares linked to trauma. Freud was partly right when he believed that dreams are for fulfillment of desires. The dream-reality work shows that this kind of dreams occurs frequently when your conscious mind strongly desires something. Consequently, if you strongly desire something, do not take your fulfillment dreams for precognitive dreams--you will be disappointed. I have observed through my work that when I strongly want something, my dreams cannot help me to anticipate the future in this regard. I lack the necessary distance and neutrality that would allow a good communication between my conscious mind and my greater consciousness. The dreams I get in this case are simply formed by my conscious mind eager to fulfill its own desires. These dreams do not stem from my greater consciousness and they are misleading. In such circumstances, I have observed that my relatives are of great help when they do not know my concerns. I ask them to tell me their dreams and most of the time they give me valuable information that could not reach my conscious mind, too much focused on strong desires. You will see through your dream-reality work that in a family it often occurs that a member will dream solutions to concerns of another member of the family. Scientists engaged in investigations should ask their family members to share their dreams. It is easy to see through the dream-reality work that some dreams are formed by the conscious mind with all its shortcomings. The more detached and neutral we are the clearer is the dream's access to information on our past, present and future. This is also true in the waking life. But distance and neutrality are not always easy!

Some persons will see that recurring nightmares show catastrophic events that (fortunately) never occur in their waking life. If this is your case, it is interesting to study this aspect through your dream-reality work. First it will show you that these are not premonitory dreams that are shaping your future but only consequences of past traumatic events. These traumas may be ancient and even may be traced back to many generations in your family. Research in psychology has shown (through group-analysis) that in some families, traumatic memory crosses generations through recurring nightmares that do not seem to be connected with the dreamers' waking life.[40] Generally these nightmares have the same emotional background and ever-changing scenery. Some dreamers may sense a strong fear, other an intense anxiety. If you are subject to these kind of nightmares, learn to detect them because you can make excellent use of them instead of just suffering. Recurring traumatic nightmares reveal that important amounts of energy is blocked in your system. Moreover, a lot of energy is wasted in the occurring of the nightmare itself and sleep is disturbed by them. Once you work on these nightmares the energy potentials are available for other purposes like higher creativity. The simultaneous observation of dreams and reality will be very useful in understanding your nightmares. After some time, you will see through your dream-reality work that some events in your waking life, a state of stress, or isolation, reactivate these powerful traumatic memories ignored by your conscious mind. More about dealing with other kinds of nightmares can be found in my book *The Intelligence of Dreams.*

You cannot change your past, but you can change and reshape your future:
Here again I am going to take the same comparison as the one I used earlier to explain why dreams anticipate the future. We have seen that the conscious mind anticipates the future and that nobody is surprised of this fact. We have also seen that the difference between the conscious mind and the greater consciousness in anticipating the future stems from the fact that much more information is available to the greater consciousness to organize its

future. Therefore, the greater consciousness can anticipate even a remote future that cannot yet be imagined by the conscious mind. For example, your greater consciousness may have programmed a trip to a country and meeting with people in this country many months before it occurs, often when you had no connections with this country and not even the slightest wish to visit.

Many times we notice in our waking life that future events that were programmed by the conscious mind finally did not happen. For example, on Monday you had taken an appointment with a friend for the next Saturday and you (or your friend) canceled the appointment on Friday. This means that until Friday, you knew your future regarding the next Saturday and yet this conscious prediction did not come true. The same can occur regarding some predictions made by the greater consciousness. It can "change its mind" and you can also make it change its mind. This is why you shouldn't be fatalistic and resigned to whatever is announced by your dreams. It is true that dreams shape your reality, but in turn your reality shapes your dreams. This is why when something you dislike is forming in the dream state you may take practical steps in your waking life to change the situation that is forming.

I am now going to speak about a technique you can use to get from your *greater consciousness* the information you want instead of simply waiting for their unmastered occurrence through dreams, intuitions and the stroke of luck.

CHAPTER 4

A powerful technique for accessing information stored in your unconscious

In this chapter I am going to speak about a technique that may be compared to "reverse engineering." Indeed, once you have decoded you dream language, it is possible not only to understand properly the messages conveyed to the conscious mind by the greater consciousness, but also to use this decoded language in order to get from the greater consciousness the information you want. In other words the dream-reality work will provide you a powerful key for accessing at will information stored in your greater consciousness.

The main reason for this heightened accessibility is that you are now trained to speak and understand the special language of your greater consciousness. And if you speak its language, your greater consciousness will better understand what you want. The language we speak in the waking life must seem alien to greater consciousness, the same way the dream language appears bizarre and nonsensical to our conscious mind. So if we try to communicate with the greater consciousness the way we speak in our waking lives, chances are that the greater consciousness won't understand us the same way most people do not understand their dreams. The greater consciousness and the conscious mind do not use the same language, even though they share some elements like words, numbers, colors and so on. As they do not speak the same language, it is difficult to efficiently pass information from one to another. With the accurate dream decoding that is made possible through the dream-reality work, this problem is solved. The greater consciousness and the conscious mind can communicate more efficiently (in other words, the two hemispheres of the brain cooperate better). As I have already explained, dreams are a bridge between the greater consciousness and the conscious mind. Once you understand the dream language, you can cross the bridge in both directions:

from the conscious mind to the greater consciousness and from the greater consciousness to the conscious mind. Pragmatically speaking, we can use the decoded dream vocabulary in two ways:

- From the greater consciousness to the conscious mind, for example to decode information transmitted by dreams: Diagram n° 9:

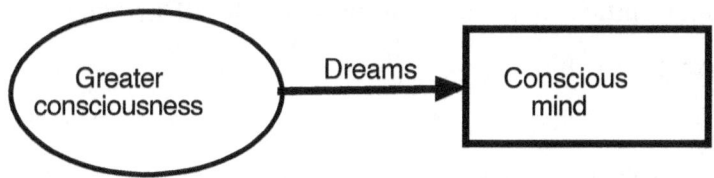

- Or from the conscious mind to the greater consciousness, for example when we want to get specific information from our greater consciousness:

Diagram n° 10:

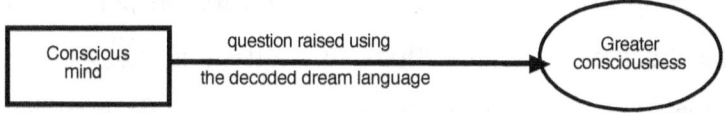

When I was conducting my own investigation about the dream process and the connections between dreams and reality, I had soon the idea to ask questions to my greater consciousness in its own language. I began asking questions to my greater consciousness by using the dream language that I had previously decoded through my dream-reality work. Before falling asleep I asked myself a question that I shaped with my decoded dream vocabulary. In so doing, I could considerably multiply opportunities to get accurate answers to all my questions through my dreams.

To illustrate this method I am going to take an example of topical interest given the current employment problems that many people are facing. If a person has decoded from his dream/reality work that the dream symbol "hat" is the symbol the most frequently used to represent her job, this person will use this same symbol the other way (that is to say from her conscious mind to her greater consciousness) to get information about her job. To do so, this person will use the dream symbol "hat" in a question she will ask herself before going to sleep. For example she may ask: "Am I going to change hats?" "Where can I get a new hat?" "Does my hat suit me?" I have noticed that this technique is more effective when I ask questions not only with words but also forming images in my mind and with strong emotion. In other words, asking a question to your greater consciousness in its specific language and forming images in your mind is a powerful way to access the information wealth of your greater consciousness. When I use this technique, my greater consciousness is never insensitive to my questions. It may answer through a dream, which will make use of the same symbols I have used in my question or of other symbols that I have also decoded through my dream-reality work. Or it may give me answers through intuitions and informative events and encounters happening apparently by pure chance in my waking life. In any case, if you use your decoded dream vocabulary to ask questions to your greater consciousness, you communicate better with it and considerably multiply the possibilities to get the information you are seeking. Your greater consciousness understands clearly what you want and it can respond with information you will understand clearly, too, because you have mastered your dream language. The greater consciousness and the conscious mind cease to be strangers and instead they cooperate, giving place to more creativity.

The conscious mind is very useful, however it would be much more efficient if it was guided and inspired by the greater consciousness, which is truly creative and more accurate. The faculties of the conscious mind are indispensable to academic research, but the conscious mind compared to the possibility of the greater consciousness is weak and more inclined to routine than to innovation.

Let us compare two kinds of researchers. Imagine two people seeking to find an old rare book. The first one would deduce from the information available (language, date of publication, nationality of the authors) in which country the book may be available. Then he would consult all the paper files or printed catalogues of all the libraries in this country or get in touch with librarians in this country to perform the search for him. This method is long, tiring and there is no guarantee of positive results. In short, it is not efficient. The other person would type the title of the book in a specialized search engine and would get the answer in a few seconds. Then he would go to that library to consult the old rare book. This method is far more efficient and is what occurs to researchers when they have been lucky enough to benefit from the help of their dreams, ideas and intuitions. The way the first person conducts his research may be compared to what happens when researchers are limited to the capabilities of their conscious mind. In this case, a lot of time and money is necessary to achieve little results.

It would be extremely interesting for researchers to learn to communicate efficiently with their greater consciousness so that they can receive answers to their questions and guidance in their research. But as I have previously stated, before you can reach this stage where you communicate easily with your greater consciousness you will need around one year of practice with the dream-reality work provided you do not block, due to the way you live, a normal communication between your conscious mind and your greater consciousness. (I will explain later on what may block this flow of information and how you can improve this flow.) Through this, you will learn how to put yourself in the best conditions to have innovative dreams, ideas and intuitions.

CHAPTER 5

The best conditions to be helped by your unconscious for your research about ancient civilizations

1. Be again in touch with your inner world

For most of us who have studied for a long time in universities, it is often difficult to access the ancient layers of the psyche because the present academic world only develops and requires the abilities of the conscious mind. Little by little this cuts us from our inner world. Our conscious mind and its memory have the answer to everything and tack upon everything new that is presented to us preconceived ideas and judgments that are admitted in the academic world and have not been challenged sometimes for centuries. Most of the mistakes made by modern researchers result from this phenomenon. All those who overload their brain with information without letting it have time to properly "digest" will hardly have dreams that stem from their unconscious. Instead, most of the time they will only have "digestive" dreams from their conscious mind, which are a mix of waking life information and nightmares. In order to get a different and more interesting kind of dream, one must limit the conscious information intake from the outer world and provide oneself with time of solitude where one can "digest" all the information received and be more receptive to one's body and its sensations. Provided you are not facing depression, I advise you to conduct this simple and interesting experiment: spend a few days alone, without TV, telephone, radio, books, etc... in a quiet place, eat little (better make a diet), and drink relaxing herbal teas. This way, you will almost always have dreams that will come from your greater consciousness.

2. Do not block the information flow between your greater consciousness and your conscious mind

To draw the maximum benefits from your sleeping time and all the information it can bring you, you should free, as much as possible, your brain from the burden of managing bodily discomfort. So, sleep in the most comfortable way possible. Avoid eating greasy food just before going to bed. This will free your brain from having to deal with messages from your stomach about digestion difficulties. It is well known that many nightmares result from digestive problems. It is easy to avoid them just by having light dinners at a time as far as possible from the time you go to bed. Studies have also shown that some medicines, drugs, and exciting substances like tea, coffee, alcohol, and tobacco may have a negative impact on the dream process. As everybody reacts differently to these substances, you should do your own experiments to know what you should avoid. As for me, I have observed that infusions of sage and lavender at night have a strong positive influence on my dream process. Lavender relaxes me and sage is well known to improve memory. The more we are relaxed at the time we go to sleep, the more opportunities we have to dream clearly and peacefully. Stress or psychological shocks before going to bed will unfortunately (if you can sleep) last once you are asleep and disturb your dream process. In this respect, you should absolutely avoid watching violent or scary movies, reading violent and scary books, or listening to the news before you go to bed. Unfortunately, all of this does not please your unconscious, which will provoke stressful dreams that will decrease your energy. One more condition matters: so that you can benefit from valuable information from your unconscious, you need to sleep long enough to recharge yourself at your maximum level of energy. Indeed, the quality of the information you can access is linked to your energy level. When your energy is low, you will not be able to access some kinds of information even if you strongly wish it. In the intangible world, you will see through your dream reality work that the law of "attraction" is implacable. In the waking life, it is easy to notice that depressed people only have dark thoughts! Try to have an energy level as high as possible; for this purpose use all the means that are available: healthy food, relaxation techniques, sports, etc... Avoid places, activities, and people that drain your energy.

3. Learn to use the time just before you fall asleep profitably

At this time, the content and the mood of your thoughts (negative or positive, sad or happy, etc...) have the property to strongly influence the content of your dreams. We can make a comparison with modern technology. These thoughts will act like key words in a search engine that will gather information from your unconscious once you are asleep. Once you are aware of this phenomenon, you can use it to ask questions to your greater consciousness in its language that you have previously decoded. When you have not yet decoded your dream language, you can do the following (it is, however, less efficient): think in a relaxed and meditative way about what you are researching. This will program your conscious mind to receive information from your unconscious on these issues while you sleep. Famous discoverers who dreamt their discoveries must have done it naturally. History of sciences shows that innovative dreams occur to people conducting research in the field of the innovative dreams during their waking state. These persons are generally passionate about their research and naturally open to messages coming from their greater consciousness through dreams and intuitions. For example, Carl Gustav Jung who worked in a field that was his calling and paid a lot of attention to his dreams, had strong opportunities to have innovative dreams. Carl Gustav Jung asserted about his researches:

> *My ideas on the centre and the Self were confirmed, later, in 1927, in a dream.[41]*

Moreover, it is through a dream in which he could see himself speaking to an audience much larger than his usual audience that he got the idea to write his book, *Man and His Symbols*.[42] Indeed, the book that is considered to be his testament was written at the end of his life and has opened this field of knowledge to the lay public. In this book, Jung quotes the novelist Robert Louis Stevenson:

> *...Having searched for many years a story that would express hidden deep feeling about the double personality of human beings, the idea of Doctor Jekyll and Mr. Hyde came to him all of a sudden in a dream.[43]*

4. Increase your life energy

Performing a dream reality work will help you increase your energy. Why? Because it helps remove psychological blocks impeding the correct circulation of energy in your body. Also because as it will help you see what decreases or increases your energy, you will be able to act consequently to change unfavorable situations and habits. Through your dream reality work you will witness more efficiently than in the waking life the variation of your energy level. An optimum level of energy gives place to dreams full of light, color, and joy. They may also be very funny and entertaining. To the contrary, fatigue and stress (and therefore low levels of energy) tend to give place to dull and uninteresting dreams. One typical dream of this kind is when before you have to travel you dream you are unable to gather all your luggage and you are stressed because it is so late and you are afraid you will miss your train or your flight. If you were not stressed you would dream instead of information about the place where you are going and the people you will meet. Thanks to the dream reality work, you will learn to detect what is good for your energy and what is bad. You will see that by staying in some places strongly decreases your energy. In this respect you will soon discover that most of the time your conscious mind and your greater consciousness do not share the same opinion at all regarding the "beauty" of places, people, animals, and objects. Through your dream reality work you will learn to better use the ability of your body to pick up good energies.

5. Sleep longer when you need to solve a difficult problem

When you cannot get a solution to a problem you are working on, don't stay stuck on it, and do not overwork. Instead take some distance by sleeping a longer time. Researchers should regularly indulge in sleep in, as sleeping longer increases the possibility to get clear dreams just before waking up. Another efficient technique to get clear dreams in the morning is to use the snooze function of your clock and to fall again in sleep between each ring. This increases your chances to get clear dreams bringing clear solutions to your problems. However the bad side of this technique is that it is tiring and should not be practiced too often.

6. Learn how to better use the properties of your body during excavations

Through your dream reality work you will see that when the body stands in an information bath it temporarily charges itself with the energy and the information of the place. Every intangible piece of information of the place is picked up by our greater consciousness, which will transfer part of it to the conscious mind through dreams and intuition. Archaeological teams would greatly benefit from paying more attention to the dreams of their members. Also, it would be a good idea to sleep several nights in the site where they intend to dig.

This way they would be able to take benefit from the ability of their body to detect information on the location of interesting things to find. The author of a book about the yoga of dreams has related this story that would make many archaeologists dream! During a trip with a group of people, he had to sleep in a site full of ruins from an ancient Shang-Shung temple in Tibet. He dreamt that he found an old garuda statuette in a mound of earth. When he woke up he filmed the ruins before leaving with the group. While he was filming he saw the mound of earth he had dreamt of. He dug and found the garuda statuette that he dreamt of. Moreover, I could observe through my teaching of the dream reality method that the more we do it the easier it is to communicate between the conscious mind and the higher the body sensitivity is to the intangible environment in the waking state. In such a way is intuition, which is nothing more than information from the greater consciousness coming to the conscious mind in the waking state, also greatly improved thanks to dream reality work. In many aspects, the greater consciousness is much more efficient and powerful than the conscious mind. But mental flexibility is required to benefit from the possibilities of the greater consciousness.

7. Make your conscious mind as flexible as possible

Our conscious mind has the bad habit of being intolerant to everything that is not in conformity with the knowledge it has accepted. This means that the more learned you are in a given field the less open you are to receive new ideas from your unconscious if you have not learned to master your conscious mind. Your conscious mind will bar you from being creative and will only let you act as a poor computer! Sometimes, it may happen that after asking a question to your greater consciousness, you have received an answer that draws smiles from your conscious mind, so that you will not even consider the information you received from the greater consciousness. How often are people with innovative ideas and intuition ridiculed by others around them and then they do not follow the road that was shown to them by their greater consciousness and proved later on to be right. When we write down our dreams, the conscious mind must be "boycotted" unless it will make fun and reject every piece of information that does not fit into its limited and strict universe. When you write down your dreams, just act as a witness; do not judge them, write down all you can remember without any judgment on what is worthy or not. Also, whenever it is possible, innovative ideas or information about archaeological sites should be checked in the waking state even if your conscious mind finds them "impossible". The more tolerantly we cooperate with the greater consciousness, the more it will pass information to the conscious mind. The opposite is also true. Before concluding this book, it is close to my heart to give advice on how to look at ancient images.

8. Learn to look at ancient images

What does a modern scholar do with an ancient picture, for example, the scene about which I have spoken at the beginning of this book?

He will promptly "label" the image. Here are the "labels" that were invented by the conscious mind of scholars, including "judgment of the dead", "weighing of the heart" and "psychostasy" (weighing of souls).

From this point, scholars' conscious minds will engulf them in written information available on the themes of death, judgment, weighing, sins, punishment, etc. They will then tack the preconceived ideas of the conscious mind and the way we see the world onto this image. Yet an ancient Egyptian picture will never deliver its information when we "look" at it this way. It will only make its information available through our unconscious mind that will then transfer its information to our conscious mind through dreams, feelings and intuitions. If scholars want to understand ancient images, they have to boycott the activities of their conscious mind (the dream-reality method will help them acquire this ability). They will then use their conscious mind during the second step to gather proofs from the written sources available. Ancient images are products widely similar to the images that are used by our unconscious mind to convey messages through our dreams. If you look at them with your conscious mind, you can only be misled. It is difficult to fully explain in words how to look at ancient images (and dream images), but this ability is easily gained by anybody taking the time to complete dream-reality work during the course of a year. Unfortunately, dream dictionaries, both ancient or modern, will not help you. You have to do your own research. Thanks to dream-reality work, you will develop a different sensitivity that unites the emotional and the rational. For those who have not yet performed dream-reality work, a powerful technique may also be used in regards to ancient images. It consists of looking at them in a relaxed way before going to sleep and doing this for several days so that these images will be impressed upon the unconscious mind. This in turn will pass the information to the conscious mind. The ancient Egyptian images, through their colors, shapes and themes, have a strong influence on our psyche. This is why, in my opinion, so many people are still fascinated by this ancient civilization and its images that are full of life. Its images, its statues, even its hieroglyphs, speak to our unconscious mind. When you look at an ancient Egyptian picture, try to forget everything you know about ancient Egypt. Look at it with new eyes, as if it were a dream symbol. Feel it. What is the general atmosphere of the picture? What is the main element? Are the actions pictured possible in the natural realm? For example, in this image, the conscious mind sees a weighing. However, the balance shown if the message was actually about a weighing would be impossible. Indeed, a heart in a vase on one pan and a feather (the symbol of Maat) on the other pan cannot result in the balance shown. The ancient Egyptians, like other ancient people (as well as our unconscious minds) were practical people. They were keen on reality and their images should be interpreted using this frame of mind. (However, in this picture, even if the message was abstract, the results shown would be impossible because a man's heart will never stand the weight of a goddess). This is why when an ancient image shows an action that is impossible on natural ground, it means that the image is used to figure something else. Here, the image does not figure a weighing—impossible action—but the existence of the relationship between human hearts and Maat (which is easily checked in all Egyptian literature). To summarize, when an action shown in an ancient image is practically impossible, you must search other avenues to discover the actual meaning of the image and the thoughts of the people who invented it. I would like to stress that we must keep in mind that ancient people had not yet developed our modern sense of abstraction. Instead, they were anchored in reality. To them, all was pragmatic reality and their perceptions of the world, as well as their thoughts, had to be translated into images that conformed with the real world. I learned this aspect in my childhood when I was my mother's "interpreter". Indeed, I had to translate the many intellectual abstractions we now use in the modern language into her real-world images. Sometimes, translation was impossible. Later on, I observed the same phenomenon in archaic Roman law. Through extensive study of the evolution of the Roman law system, it was possible to witness the step-by-step evolution towards our modern collective psyche. Initially, law was grounded in tangible reality, but little by little lawyers have built a universe of abstractions (legal fictions) that they today take as legal realities. I am going to use the example of the right of property to illustrate this phenomenon. In archaic Roman law, it was necessary to physically hold a thing in order to have the property of it. Similarly, it was necessary to pass it to another person in order to transfer the property. Property was a power exerted on a thing and the modern concept of **right** of property did not yet exist. It was invented a long time later. It made possible the legal practice permitting the transfer of ownership of a thing without transferring the thing itself at the same time. In other words, law made it possible to transfer property through transferring only a piece of paper that had been signed. Finally, lawyers came to invent the concept of "incorporeal property", or property that is no longer built on tangible things but on ideas and rights. This would have been inconceivable to the archaic Roman "priests-layers" because the right of incorporeal property (even the simple **right** of property) did not exist in the realm of nature. Try to picture the right of incorporeal property, or even simply a right! It is impossible.

CONCLUSION

Dream-reality work will lead you step-by-step in understanding the mental universe of ancient people. You will understand that they lived in a different mental universe, mainly because their bodies instinctively perceived the energy of places, persons, animals and objects. This is why the intangible side of life was important to them. Although we have lost this ability in the waking state, some of it is still available in the dream state; discovering it through dream reality work is the best way to understand the concerns of people who looked at the world in a manner that is so alien to our materialistic approach. Seeing the world with their eyes will allow researchers to answer many questions and improve the translations of ancient texts. This change of perspective will permit us to solve many "enigmas" that are such only because the conscious mind of modern people perceive and consider only half the dimension of reality, while ancient people perceived the intangible, the tangible and their connections as a whole. While we believe that wealth is material, ancient people understood that true abundance came from an abundance of life energy. When the symbolic way they used to speak and portray their knowledge is understood, it is possible to find in their archeological remains their wisdom and their knowledge of nature and of the human psyche our civilization has not yet reached, despite our technological advances. Through my research on what we consider ancient legal systems, it is obvious to me that civilizations that were much more developed than ours have lived on our planet. They seemed to know how to perfectly manage and use different cosmic energies, especially solar energy, for their daily life purposes. I believe that ancient Egypt, who exerts a strong fascination on us, has brought to the modern world only bits of a previous knowledge that for now is still beyond the reach of modern intelligence.

BIBLIOGRAPHY

Aristotle, *La Vérité des songes, De la divination dans le sommeil*, (Parva naturalia 462 b - 464 b), translated and presented by Jackie Pigeaud, Paris, Rivages Poche, 1995

Artemidorus, *The Interpretation of Dreams: Oneirocritica*, Translated by R. J. White, Park Ridge, N.J., Noyes Press, 1975

E. R. Dodds, *Les Grecs et l'irrationnel*, Paris, Aubier, 1965. "Supernormal phenomena in Classical Antiquity", in *The Ancient Concept of Progress and other Essays on Greek Literature and Belief*, Clarendon Press, Oxford, 1973

Changeux Jean-Pierre, *Neuronal Man, The Biology of Mind*, New York, Oxford, Oxford University Press, 1986
DOSSEY Larry, *Reinventing Medicine: Beyond Mind-Body To A New Era Of Healing*, New York, Haper Collins, 1999.

Freud Sigmund, *The Interpretation of Dreams*, New York: Avon Books, 1965 (first publication in 1900)

Hobson J. Allen, *The Dreaming Brain*, Penguin, 1990 (Scientific approach)

Jung Carl Gustav, *Memories, Dreams and Reflections*, London, Routledge and Kegan paul, 1963

Norbu NamKhai, *Dream Yoga and the Practice of Natural Light*, New York, Snow Lion Publications, 1992. (French translation Le *Yoga du Rêve*, Paris, J.L. Accarias, 1993, collection L'originel, translation by arrangement with Snow Lion Publications, Ithaca, New York 14851, Editor KATZ, Michel translation by GAUDEBERT Gisèle

Woods Ralph L. and Greenhouse Herbert B., Editors, *The New World of Dreams*, New York, Macmillan Publishing Co, inc., second printing 1974,

NOTES

[1] Siegfried Morenz, *Egyptian Religion*, London, Methuen and Co ltd, 1976, p. 126-127.
[2] R. O. Faulkner, *The Ancient Egyptian Book of the Dead*, London, British Museum Press, p. 31.
[3] R. O. Faulkner, *The Ancient Egyptian Book of the Dead*, London, British Museum Press, p. 34.
[4] Etienne Drioton, "Le jugement des âmes dans l'Egypte ancienne", Revue du Caire, 1949, p. 1-2. Translated from French: « Un monstre à l'allure d'hippopotame, la Dévorante, accroupi auprès de la balance, attend que le damné lui soit livré en pâture."
[5] Erik Hornung, *L'esprit du temps des pharaons*, op. cit., p. 57, translated from French: "Après l'époque armanienne, on y ajoutera encore l'image de la 'Dévorante' incarnant la gueule de l'enfer."
[6] Moustafa Gadalla, *Egyptian Divinities - The All Who Are the One*, Tehuti Research Foundation, August 21, 2001, p.102.
[7] Luther Link, *Devil: A Mask without a Face*, Reaktion Books, p. 115
[8] Lila Perl Yerkow, Mummies, Tombs, and Treasure: Secrets of Ancient Egypt, Clarion Books, p. 74
[9] Robert A. Armour, *Gods and Myths of Ancient Egypt*, AUC Press, p. 141.

[10] Sören Kierkegaard, *Traité du désespoir*, Paris, Gallimard, Folio Essais, 1949, p. 61, p. 87 and p. 89.

[11] Information found in Changeux Jean-Pierre, *Neuronal Man, The Biology of Mind*, New York, Oxford, Oxford University Press, 1986, Originally published in France as *L'homme Neuronal* by Fayard, Paris, 1983, p. 60. On the use of the electroencephalograph in dream laboratories, see: *The New World of Dreams*, New York, Macmillan Publishing Co, inc., second printing 1974, p. 278.

[12] http://www.fondation-altran.org
http://www.wadsworth.org

[13] Jonathan R. Wolpaw, Niels Birbaumer, Dennis J. McFarland, Gert Pfurtscheller, Theresa m. Vaugan, *Brain-computer interfaces for communication and control*, Clinical Neurophysiology, volume 113, Issue 6, June 2002, pages 767-791.

[14] According to Georges Hadjo, researches in electrography took place as early as 1900 and Semyon Kirlian was not aware of the results of his predecessors: Carsten in England and Henri Baraduc and Lodko Narkiewiez in Paris in 1896, see his interesting article "L'effet Kirlian," in *Bio Contact*, Gaillac, France, n° 112, March 2002, biocontact@wanadoo.fr. See: Lindgren C. E. (Editor), *Capturing the Aura: Integrating Science, Technology and Metaphysics*, Blue Dolphin Pub, June 2000; Krippner Stanley and Rubin Daniel, *Kirlian Aura*, Garden City. N.Y., Doubleday & Co, 1974. *The Human Aura in Acupuncture and Kirlian Photography* (Social Change Series), By Acupuncture and Western hemisphere Conference on Kirlian Photography, Gordon and Breach Science Pub; 1974.

[15] Bernard Guérin, *Bioénergétique*, EDP sciences, 2004.

[16] Democritus believed that we pick up, through the skin, images emitted by objects and people. He believed that these images conveyed emotions. See: J.P. Dumont, *Les Présocratiques*, Paris, Pléïade, Folio Essai, 1988, p. 542,

quoted by Jackie Pigeaud in her observations on the translation of *La Vérité des songes* by Aristotle, *op. cit.* Ancient books on dreams have not conveyed comprehensive studies about research on the connections between the tangible and the intangible during the dreaming process. The authors of antiquity were too much focused on dream interpretation with a practical aim and on foretelling the future. Moreover, it seems that these authors, like other people, neglected their own self-observation of the dreaming process. Aristotle does not show through his writing a sound knowledge of this phenomenon. Inner observation of self was not the basis of Artemidorus' works on dream interpretation. Artemidorus was very famous for his dream dictionary, (Artemidorus, *The Interpretation of Dreams: Oneirocritica*, Translated by White R. J., Park Ridge, N.J., Noyes Press, 1975). Artemidorus did not consider the dreaming process in a wider life context including both the tangible and the intangible worlds. All the authors, modern or ancient, are too focused on the content of dreams and not open to the realities that would allow a better understanding of the dreaming process. In ancient Egypt, people and magicians were also interested in dreams, mainly for foretelling the future, as Wallis-Budge has stated. He also wrote that the Egyptian magicians had invented spells to receive dreams on the future. He quotes the Papyrus n° 122 of the British Museum, line 64 *ff.* and line 359 *ff.*, in his article: E. A Wallis-Budge, "Dream magic of Ancient Egypt," 129-130, *The New World of Dreams*, *op. cit.*

[17] In the same line, see: Dossey Larry, *Reinventing Medicine: Beyond Mind-Body To A New Era Of Healing*, New York, Harper Collins, 1999, p. 80.

[18] Aldous Huxley, *The Doors of Perception, and Heaven and Hell*, Vintage, 2004, p. 10.
[19] John Locke, *An Essay Concerning Human Understanding*, Penguin Books, 1997, p. 3.
[20] On the conscious mind acting as a filter of information see: Chet B. Snow, Helen Wambach, *Vision du futur de l'humanité*, op. cit., p. 64.
[21] Christiane Desroches-Noblecourt, *Le fabuleux héritage de l'Egypte*, Editions S. W. Télémaque, Paris, 2007, p. 291.
[22] On this topic see: Eggan Dorothy, "The Culture Shapes the Dream," p. 120-124, *op. cit.*
[23] For example: Chevalier Jean, Gheerbrant Alain, *Dictionnaire des Symboles*, Laffont, Jupiter, collection Bouquins, Paris, 1982. Or on the symbols of "moon" or "water" see: Eliade Mircea, *Une nouvelle philosophie de la Lune*, Paris, L'Herne, 2001.
[24] Isolation is not advised to depressed people.
[25] Other techniques are listed in the *Intelligence of dreams*, op. cit, question n° 1.
[26] For examples of dreams announcing death and for examples of warning dreams see: Kelsey Morton, *Dreams: A Way to Listen to God*, New York/Mahwah, Paulist Press, 1989, p. 13, p. 44, p. 72, p. 74 and p. 79. See also: *The New World of Dreams*, op. cit., p. 132.
[27] Galen, *On diagnosis from Dreams*, Translation by Oberhelman T., J. Histoire médicale 38, 1983, p. 36-47; Hippocrate, *Du Régime*, translation by Joly R., Paris, Belles Lettres, 1967.
[28] Taken from the DVD about the exhibition: Sunken Cities of Egypt:
[29] Descartes René, *Discours de la Méthode*, Paris, GF Flammarion, 1966, p 208, original text: *"Un moment après, il eut un troisième songe... il trouva un livre sur sa*

table, sans savoir qui l'y avait mis. Il l'ouvrit et voyant que c'était un Dictionnaire, il en fut ravi dans l'espérance qu'il pourrait lui être fort utile. Dans le même instant, il se rencontra un autre livre sous sa main, qui ne lui était pas moins nouveau, ne sachant d'où il lui était venu. Il trouva que c'était un recueil des Poésies de différents auteurs, intitulé Corpus Poëtarum etc. Il eut la curiosité d'y vouloir lire quelque chose: et à l'ouverture du livre, il tomba sur le vers Quod Vitae sectabor iter? (= quelle voie suivrai-je en la vie?).

[30] See Moss Robert's examples about psychic litter in hotels, *Dreamgates, op. cit.*, p. 216

[31] For examples quoted by a modern doctor, see: Dossey Larry, *Reinventing Medicine, op.cit.*, p. 123.

[32] Mancini Anna, *The Intelligence of Dreams*, Buenos Books America, Dover, 2003

[33] This experiment should not be performed by depressed people.

[34] Nina Berberova, *C'est moi qui souligne*, traduit du Russe par Anne and René Misslin, Paris, J'ai lu, p. 447.

[35] http://en.wikipedia.org/wiki/Akashic_Records

[36] See for example the papyrus of Hunefer, British Museum, 9901/3. As E. A. Wallis-Budge has explained: Thoth "was considered to be the possessor of all knowledge both human and divine." E. A. Wallis Budge, *Egyptian Magic*, Arkana, 1988, p. 128.

[37] Some authors noticed the same, see for example: Moss Robert, *Dreaming True, How to Dream Your Future and Change Your Life for the Bette*r, New York, Pocket Books, September 2000, p. 29 et p. 189; and by the same author, *Dreamgates*, p. 17-19; Dee Nerys, *Your Dreams and what They Mean*, London and San Francisco, Thorsons, 1984, p. 85.

[38] *Cf.* note n° 26.

[39] Isabel Allende asserts that through her dreams she could anticipate when she would be pregnant and the gender of the baby to be born. Later on she was able to use this ability for her relatives. Allende Isabel, *Paula*, Paris, Fayard, 1995, p. 158. See also on dreams anticipating pregnancies: Malinowski Bronislaw, "The dream is the Cause of the Wish," p.118-119: "Another class of typical dream is concerned with the birth of babies. In these the future mother has a sort of dream annunciation from one of her dead relatives." in Ralph L. Woods and Herbert B. Greenhouse, Editors, *The New World of Dreams*, New York, Macmillan Publishing Co, inc., second printing 1974, p. 119.

[40] More information on nightmares in *The Intelligence of Dreams*, see in the Frequently Asked Questions the section about psychological nightmares.

[41] Carl Gustav Jung "Ma vie", Collections Témoins Gallimard, p. 229, translated from French: *"Mes idées sur le centre et sur le Soi me furent confirmées plus tard, en 1927, par un rêve"*.

[42] Carl Gustav Jung, Essai d'exploration de l'inconscient, in English: *Man and His Symbols*, Picador, 1978

[43] Carl Gustav Jung, *Essai d'exploration de l'inconscient*, Coll. Folio Essais, n° 90, p. 61, translated from French: *"...ayant cherché pendant des années une histoire qui exprimerait le sentiment profond qu'il avait d'une double personnalité de l'être humain, Le docteur Jekyll et Mr Hyde, lui fut soudain révélé en rêve"*.

Other books by Anna Mancini, Ph. D:

MAAT REVEALED,
Philosophy of Justice in Ancient Egypt,
by Anna Mancini Ph. D
ISBN: 9781932848106

ANCIENT ROMAN
SOLUTIONS
TO MODERN LEGAL ISSUES,
THE EXAMPLE OF PATENT LAW
ISBN: 9781932848045

THE INTELLIGENCE OF DREAMS
ISBN: 9781932848021

SCIENTIFIC CREATIVITY
ISBN: 9781932848243

www.ingramcontent.com/pod-product-compliance
Lightning Source LLC
Chambersburg PA
CBHW021846220426
43663CB00005B/419